SEOUL

A Curated Guide: SEOUL

Published in 2018 by Seoul Selection U.S.A., Inc.
4199 Campus Drive, Suite 550, Irvine, CA 92612
Phone: 949-509-6584 / Seoul office: 82-2-734-9567
Fax: 949-509-6599 / Seoul office: 82-2-734-9562
Email: hankinseoul@gmail.com

ISBN: 978-1-62412-120-3 52800
Library of Congress Control Number: 2018963746

Printed in the Republic of Korea

A Curated Guide

SEOUL

Written by Robert Koehler and Hahna Yoon

Seoul Selection

Introduction

Often, a city's true charm lies not in its over-trodden attractions. In Seoul, strolling through its narrow alleyways or sampling delicacies at its hidden holes-in-the-wall can leave a more profound impression than merely hopping from one landmark to the next. "Seoul: A Curated Guide" is no point-by-point directory of everything Korea's historic capital has to offer. Rather, it is - as the title suggests - a curated selection, one that focuses on local favorites, destinations and activities often missing from print and online top ten lists. Here you'll find the neighborhoods and locations that locals themselves explore and enjoy, the places and spaces that made us - the writers of this humble guide - fall in love with this city in the first place.

Contents

Neighborhoods

Seochon 서촌

 Gyeongbokgung, Line 3

Nestled between Gyeongbokgung Palace and the western slopes of Inwangsan Mountain, Seochon is a soothing medley of art, history, nature and fun. In the days of Joseon (1392–1910), a mix of royals, aristocrats and middle-class families called the area home. In the early 20th century, the neighborhood's quiet alleys and misty mountains provided solace and inspiration to many of the country's most celebrated artists and writers. The artistic heritage lives on today in the many museums, galleries and art spaces hidden in the low-rise district's web of narrow alleyways.

Along with Bukchon and Ikseon-dong, Seochon boasts one of the city's largest collections of traditional tile roof homes, or *hanok*. Though many of these houses are still residential, a growing number now serve as cafés, restaurants, boutiques and workshops. These homes give the district its distinctly vintage ambiance.

Seochon isn't a bad place to eat, either. You'll find plenty of great places to eat on the so-called **Sejong Village Food Street**. **Tosokchon Samgyetang**, the city's best known place to get chicken and ginseng soup, or *samgyetang*, is also in Seochon.

Art Spaces

Seochon's art scene embraces big corporate museums, small independent galleries and everything in between. An exhaustive list would be impossible—we'll just share with you some of our favorites.

Seochon's most popular arts space is the **Daelim Museum**, which you can read more about in our Culture section (p. 77). Facing Gyeongbokgung, on the road to the presidential mansion, is **Tonguidong BoanYeogwan** ②, a colonial era inn where many renowned artists and writers boarded. It now hosts exhibits of an often experimental nature. Just next door is **Artspace Boan1942**, a newly built wing with more exhibition space, a bookstore and a café.

The **Park No-soo Art Museum** was the home of the late painter Park No-soo (1927–2013), who brought a modern touch to traditional ink paintings. The stately house, built in 1938 and purchased by Park in 1973, combines Korean, Chinese and Western architecture. On exhibit are about 1,000 works of art—Park's own work and his personal collection.

A beautifully repurposed *hanok*, the **I Sang's House** ① serves as both a memorial to avant-garde writer Yi Sang (1910–1937) and a public lounge.

Fans of photography should stop by
both the **Ryugaheon Gallery**, where
there's always something interesting
on exhibit, and **Irasun** ⑤, a bookstore
dedicated to photo books and a
personal favorite of this writer.

Cafés and Bakeries

A neighborhood this artsy naturally has
plenty of cafés in which to waste an
afternoon.

A favorite of this writer is **MK2** ③,
called "Seochon's Bauhaus" by one
local lifestyle magazine. Popular with
artists and designers, this space is a
little piece of Berlin with mid-century
furnishings, a tiny alcove with art books,
a good coffee menu and a view of the
hanok across the street through the
plate glass window.

Ohoo Café is a pleasant, well-lit and
minimalistly appointed space with big
windows through which to watch life
pass by. **Club Spectre** is a tiny space,

but its vintage furniture and artistically presented beverages and coffee have made it an Instagram favorite.

Need a snack? **Hyoja Bakery** ④ is a neighborhood bakery that has been supplying the presidential mansion with bread and cakes since 1987. They do bread the old-school Korean way—a bit sweet, with popular items including red bean buns and rolls baked with diced onion and corn. **Tongin Sweet**, meanwhile, is a hole-in-the-wall shop that does lovely Portuguese egg tarts.

Ogin Oraksil 옥인오락실

This old video game arcade has been around in one form or another since the 1980s. You'll find some of your favorite classic games here, including *Tetris*, *Street Fighter* and *Bubble Bobble*.

Ikseon-dong 익선동

 Jongno 3-ga, Line 1, 3, 5

Founded by real estate developer and independence activist Jeong Se-gwon in the 1920s, Ikseon-dong is the city's oldest *hanok* neighborhood, predating better-known ones such as Bukchon and Seochon. It's one of the hottest spots in the city, too, its narrow, picturesque alleyways and its trendy, Insta-ready eateries drawing endless crowds. Few places blend traditional Korean charm and contemporary sophistication so well.

Seen from above, Ikseon-dong resembles a lake of roof tiles surrounded by the high-rises of Jongno. Just a couple of years ago, this maze of alleyways was decidedly run-down, its homes dilapidated, the entire district seemingly destined for the redeveloper's wrecking ball. Then it got discovered. And gentrified.

The best way to explore Ikseon-dong is to simply wander around, getting lost in its alleyways. Every corner reveals something new. Though many of Ikseon-dong's establishments cater to the young and hip, you can find more rustic hospitality, too, especially around Jongno 3-ga Station, where there are plenty of barbecue joints, hangover soup places and soju and *makgeolli* pubs.

Restaurants and Cafés

Most people come to Ikseon-dong for the eats. Many of the historical *hanok* homes and old commercial spaces have been converted into restaurants and cafés, delightful blends of the vintage and the chic. You'll find everything here, from places that do simple Korean street food to Italian dining, French bakeries and cafés making artisanal ice cream. It's easy to figure out where the popular places are—just look for the lines.

Here are a few places to get you started. The hottest of the hot is

"When I opened this tea house in Ikseon-dong, almost by accident, in 2009, it was a very quiet place. Starting two or three years ago, though, shops started opening here, and now it's a hot spot. From my perspective, it's a miracle. Even if we don't always agree on things, I still hope everyone's business flourishes."

- Kim Ae-ran, Tteuran

probably **Gyeongyangsik 1920**, where the classic interior compliments the Japanese-style pork cutlets, hamburg steak and wine. **Yeoldudal** ①②, meanwhile, not only serves lovely pasta dishes, but also has a market selling artisanal foodstuffs. Healthy eaters should try **Ikseondong 121**, where the menu includes soy bean stew *bibimbap* and a variety of delicious curries, including chicken breast mango curry and lentil curry. **Dongnama** does Thai cuisine in vintage surroundings. For good Korean street food, try **ChangHwaDang**. **Peuangdi** proffers some lovely macarons, while **Seoul Coffee** does some fine ice cream and other desserts. For something really retro, get yourself a can of beer and some grilled fish at **Geobugi (Turtle) Supermarket**.

Two highly recommended spots, the café **Sikmul** and tea house **Tteuran**, have their own write-ups in the café section (p. 151, 157).

Barbecue Joints ❸

Though much of Ikseon-dong has gentrified, one part that's still pretty old-school is the area around Jongno 3-ga Station. This is where you'll find plenty of meat restaurants that do a roaring trade after sunset. Most of these places double as watering holes, where you can wash down your barbecued meat with a shot or five of soju.

Nakwon Arcade 낙원상가 ❹

Not actually part of Ikseon-dong but close enough, the aging Nagwon Arcade is the biggest musical instrument market in the country, if not the world. Crowded into two floors are around 300 musical instrument shops selling everything from traditional Korean musical instruments like *gayageum* zithers to electric guitars. Surrounding the arcade are many old rice cake shops. Also in the alleys nearby are a number of bars and cafés catering to the city's LGBT community.

Seongbuk-dong 성북동

 Hansung Univ., Line 4

"Seongbuk" means "north of the city wall," and in this, there is truth in advertising. Seongbuk-dong is a quiet, leafy, mostly residential neighborhood tucked away in the hills just north of Seoul's old city wall. Drawn by the peaceful vibe, clean air and mountain scenery, many of Seoul's well-to-do call the area home. So do many diplomats, giving the neighborhood an unexpected hint of the cosmopolitan.

The neighborhood boasts plenty of history and culture, too. Hidden in the hills and forests are stately old homes and beautiful gardens, left behind by the writers and artists who have lived here over the centuries. Though currently closed for renovation, the historical Kansong Art Museum boasts one of the finest collections of Korean classical art, a collection that includes no fewer than 12 listed national treasures. You'll also find plenty of time-honored eateries and charming cafés at which to refresh and relax.

Choi Sunu House 최순우 옛집 ❶

Built in the 1930s, this beautiful *hanok* was the home of renowned art historian Choi Sunu, the fourth director of the National Museum of Korea from 1974 to his death in 1984. Inside, the home has a simple, unpretentious beauty. Outside, its lovely courtyard and garden make perfect spots to repose. The home displays Choi's personal items and hosts special exhibits, musical performances and other cultural events.

Suyeon Sanbang 수연산방 ❷ ❸

One of the best teahouses in the city is also the former home of writer Yi Tae-jun (1904–unknown), whose mastery of the short story draws comparisons to Guy de Maupassant. Yi designed the house himself, whimsical elements such as the smiling dogs in the wooden railings testifying to his sense of humor.

Yi defected to North Korea in 1946, but his descendants still own the perfectly preserved home, which they converted into a teahouse that serves excellent traditional teas, beverages, rice cakes and Korean desserts. If it's open, sit in the raised pavilion overlooking the garden.

Gilsangsa Temple 길상사 ❹

Tucked away in a forest on the lower slopes of Bugaksan Mountain, Gilsangsa isn't your typical Buddhist monastery. It used to be a *yojeong*, a high-class restaurant where *gisaeng*—young women highly trained in traditional music and dance—

entertained high-powered guests such as politicians and business leaders. In 1987, the owner Kim Yeong-han, herself a former *gisaeng*, offered the property to the beloved Buddhist monk Beopjeong. In 1995, he accepted the donation, transforming it into a temple. Unlike most temples, which have brightly painted buildings, Gilsangsa's halls are rustic and unpainted, evidencing its past.

With its forests and streams, Gilsangsa offers the weary traveler a welcome space in which to recharge. There's a public meditation hall, but even better is the outdoor meditation space overlooking a deep ravine. The temple hosts an active Templestay program, too.

Bukjeong Village 북정마을 ❻

On a hill overlooking Seongbuk-dong's main road, just below Seoul's old city wall, is a community of narrow, winding alleys lined by simple, one-story homes. Called Bukjeong Village, the hamlet is a throwback to Seoul's more hardscrabble past, when such working-class, hillside neighborhoods were common throughout the city. Though the community is mostly residential, you'll find a few cafés, workshops and exhibit spaces, too.

Just above Bukjeong Village is a section of the old city wall. A trail follows the wall from Bukjeong Village to Waryong Park, where you can enjoy views of downtown Seoul. Just below Bukjeong Village, meanwhile,

is the **Simujang** ⑤, the former home of Buddhist monk, poet and independence activist Han Yong-un (1879–1944), better known by his pen name, Manhae. The simple *hanok* and garden with a couple of beautiful old trees offer shade in which to rest.

Euljiro 을지로

 Euljiro 3-ga, Line 2, 3

Euljiro, along with nearby Myeong-dong, constitutes Seoul's old commercial core. Whereas Myeong-dong has gone glitzy, however, Euljiro is a space of contrasts, where the steel and glass towers of investment banks give way to low-rise districts of rusting factories and gritty alleyways. This is where 20th century industrial capitalism and 21st century financial capitalism meet, jarringly.

Like similar districts in cities elsewhere, Euljiro's distinctively urban allure, relatively low rents and downtown convenience are attracting young entrepreneurs and creatives. Hidden away amid the industrial facilities and aging commercial blocks, mixing in with the old restaurants, metalworking shops, lighting merchants and computer repairmen, are retro cafés, hipster bars, vintage shops and ateliers. In particular, the recent renovation of the Sewoon Shopping Center, a crumbling 50-year-old mega structure, may bring big changes to the area in the immediate future.

Sewoon Shopping Center 세운상가

When it was completed in the late 1960s, the Sewoon Shopping Center was the largest concrete structure in East Asia, four massive mixed-use blocks of seven to 13 stories each. In the 1980s, it was the center of the country's trade in home electronics, computers and pirated software. By the 2000s, however, it had become an eyesore. In 2014, the city announced it would turn the crumbling site into a "makers' city" bringing together existing industries and emerging technologies, a place where people from all walks of life could come, tinker and create.

> "In order to really know a person, you should see what's inside them over a long time. Likewise, with Seoul, with Euljiro, in the maze of alleys, you can find a 'real,' decades-old vibe. The people living and working in the alleys, these unadorned scenes—that's the real Korea."
>
> —Kang Yun-seok, Coffee Hanyakbang

The first stage of this project was completed in 2017. The arcade's electronics merchants are still there, but joining them are workrooms for startups, robotics labs, independent bookstores, exhibit spaces and cafés with long lines in front of them. The open rooftop not only offers inspiring views over downtown Seoul, but also hosts concerts, festivals and other events.

Old Restaurants

Euljiro boasts many time-honored eateries, some catering to workers from local offices and factories, others favored by a wider ground. The list includes **Woo Lae Oak** (see p. 99), serving outstanding Pyeongyang-style chilled noodles (*naengmyeon*) since 1946; **Munhwaok**, a beef broth soup (*seolleongtang*) joint with over 60 years of history; **Dongwonjip**, a pork and potato stew (*gamjatang*) place first opened in 1987; **Jeonjuok**, a popular ribs joint for decades; and the Chinese restaurants **Andongjang** and **Ogubanjeom**, founded in 1948 and 1953, respectively. There are a lot more, too—just wander around the alleyways and explore.

At night, swing by the so-called **Nogari Alley**, where you'll find some boisterous old-school bars serving cheap draft beer and even cheaper dried pollack a.k.a. *nogari*.

Hip Cafés and Bars

Creatives are injecting the neighborhood with a bit of youthful energy. In the Sewoon Shopping Center, **Horangii Coffee** not only does a mean latte, but makes a fine bahn mi sandwich, too.

One place that's helped turn Euljiro into a hot spot is **Coffee Hanyakbang**. Hidden in a very narrow, very gritty

Coffee Hanyakbang

을지맥옥 Euljiro Brewing Craft Beer

alleyway, the café brings to mind old Hong Kong with its location and antique furnishings. It operates a similarly vintage dessert shop in the same alleyway.

Located on the fourth floor of an old office in the printing district, **Hotel Soosunhwa** is part café, part workshop, part showroom, run by a trio of female designers. It's a great spot to break out the laptop and do some work.

No discussion of Euljiro's hip side would be complete without mention of **Seendosi**, a hip bar similarly hidden on the top floor of an aging office building. Read more about it on p. 171.

Eulji Yuram 을지유람

The best way to explore the Euljiro area is to follow the so-called Eulji Yuram, an urban walking trail drawn up by the local government. The trail takes you through Euljiro's maze of old metalworking shops, tile and pipe stores, lighting market, the Sewoon Shopping Center, Nogari Alley and more. It's like walking into Seoul of the 1980s. Just follow the red signs on the pavement and you won't get lost.

Seoullo 7017 and Its Environs 서울로 주변

 Seoul Station, Line 1, 4

The opening of Seoullo 7017 in 2017 marked the start of a new era for downtown Seoul. By transforming a disused overpass into an elevated urban park, the project not only gave the area around Seoul Station a major facelift, but also injected some much needed vigor into what had been a relatively neglected part of the city.

In addition to the new, the area around Seoullo 7017 has plenty of old. You can find some of Seoul's most iconic works of historical architecture, including old Seoul Station (introduced in the Architecture section). Covering the hillsides behind the station are mazes of residential alleyways in which are hidden old markets, shops that have been in business for generations and picturesque communities overlooking Namsan Mountain. To explore this area is to go back to a simpler time, a time when Seoul was a city of wood, brick and concrete, not glass and steel.

Seoullo 7017 서울로 7017

Often likened to New York's High Line, Seoullo 7017 has preserved a piece of Seoul's history and given residents and visitors a space to relax, have a cuppa and take in the views.

The Seoul Station Overpass, built in 1970 to help alleviate traffic conditions around the station, was closed to traffic in 2015 after it was deemed unsafe. Rather than bulldoze the old road, however, Seoul Metropolitan Government decided to transform it into an elevated pedestrian walkway connecting the commercial Namdaemun area with the residential districts behind Seoul Station. The city commissioned Dutch architecture house MVRDV with turning the kilometer stretch of road into a garden in the sky.

The result, Seoullo 7017, opened on May, 2017. Taking its name from the year when the overpass was

constructed (1970) and the year the new park opened (2017), the walkway boasts over 13,000 trees, plants and flowers, mostly in concrete cylindrical planters. Blue lights illuminate the overpass at night.

Besides the greenery, Seoullo 7017 has cafés, snack shops and observation decks overlooking the Seoul Station and Namdaemun areas.

Sungnyemun Gate 숭례문

One of the city's most iconic pieces of traditional architecture, Sungnyemun Gate was the southern portal ("Namdaemun") through Seoul's old city wall in the days of Joseon. The stone gate topped with a two-story superstructure of wood was originally built in 1398. In 1907, however, the Japanese demolished the walls flanking the gate, ostensibly to make way for road and tram development, turning the venerable gateway into a traffic island, a condition it would have to endure until 2005, when a public park was constructed around it. Though a 2008 arson attack seriously damaged the

wooden superstructure, the gate was reopened to the public in 2013 after an extensive multi-year restoration in which sections of the old city wall were rebuilt.

One of city's oldest and largest traditional markets, the sprawling Namdaemun Market, developed just outside the old portal.

Yakhyeon Catholic Church 약현성당

Completed in 1892, the Yakhyeon Catholic Church is the oldest Western-style house of Christian worship in Korea. French missionaries built the pretty Gothic and Romanesque church just outside Sungnyemun Gate atop a hill covered in medicinal herbs, a

yakhyeon. The church also overlooks Seosomun Martyrs' Shrine, where around 100 Catholics were executed during a series of anti-Catholic persecutions in the 19th century.

Malli-dong and Cheongpa-dong
만리동과 청파동

The opening of Seoullo 7017 has encouraged people to explore the area around Seoul Station, especially the hillside districts of Malli-dong and Cheongpa-dong. One architecture scholar called the jumble of colonial Japanese-style homes, later Korean-style homes, brick houses from the 1970s and newer low-cost apartments from the 1980s a "museum of 20th century housing." One piece of local history is **Gaemi Supermarket**, a grocery store with 120 years of history. Another fascinating living museum

is the Malli Market's beautifully ramshackle **Seong-u Barber Shop** ①, which has been in operation since 1927.

This area has a bit of the hip, too. Malli-dong's **HyunSangSo** ② used to be a photo processing lab, but now it's an elegant café and exhibit space. Operated by a furniture designer in a century-old stone house, **Very Street Kitchen** ③ serves street cuisine from around the world and innovative takes on Korean traditional cuisine. The intimate pub **Reasonable Kitchen**, meanwhile, does excellent spicy chicken stew, or *dakbokkeumtang*.

For a bit of culture, swing by the **Baik-Chang Theater** ④, home to the National Theater Company of Korea. Formerly a military base, the bright red complex of containers and remodeled warehouses and garages hosts regular performances and workshops.

Gyeongnidan-gil and Haebangchon

경리단길과 해방촌

 Noksapyeon, Line 6

A bit gritty and plenty cool, the Gyeongnidan-gil neighborhood has a cosmopolitan ambiance all its own, the result of so many expats and globe-trotting Koreans who have opened places here. Over the last three years, the place has gone from being a quiet, nondescript residential district off the multicultural shopping and entertainment district of Itaewon to becoming a byword for gentrification.

Facing Gyeongnidan-gil, just across the main road to the Namsan Tunnel 3, is Haebangchon, or "Liberation Village," a hillside neighborhood founded by refugees from North Korea and Koreans returning from overseas following Korea's liberation from colonial rule in 1945. Much more recently, it was a popular residential district for Korea's international community. Like Gyeongnidan-gil, however, it's currently in the middle of a cultural boom, its streets and alleys lined by an ever-growing number of restaurants, bars, cafés, art spaces and bookstores. But unlike Gyeongnidan-gil, which has reached the point of saturation, Haebangchon's rise has only just begun.

Gyeongnidan-gil 경리단길

Gyeongnidan-gil follows the kilometer-long street running up Namsan Mountain from the headquarters of the Armed Forces Financial Management Corps—the Gyeongnidan, from which the street gets its name—to the Hyatt Hotel. More broadly speaking, however, it encompasses the entire area north of Noksapyeong Station and east of the road to Namsan Tunnel 3.

You could do a guidebook on Gyeongnidan-gil alone. Places this writer enjoys include **The Baker's Table**, a German bakery/bistro; **Kkaolli Pochana**, a hole-in-the-wall serving some of the best Thai food in the city; quiet café **Berkeley Coffee Social**; Australian brunch café **Summer Lane**; cigar club **Burn in Hal**; and café/art space/anti-gentrification movement hub **Takeout Drawing**.

Gyeongnidan-gil is also holy ground to Korean beer fans. Places such as **Craftworks**, **Magpie** and **Booth** jumpstarted Korea's craft beer scene. All three are still going strong today. Worth checking out is **Woori Super**, a former neighborhood convenience store that now has one of the city's widest selections of local and imported craft brews.

Itaewon Foreign Bookstore

This piece of history near Noksapyeong
Station has an extensive, eclectic
and absolutely fascinating collection
of used English-language books,
from Stephen King best-sellers to
discarded US Army field manuals.
The proprietor, who began collecting
English-language books from US
Army dumps in the 1960s, opened the
store in 1973. You could easily kill an
afternoon here exploring the shelves,

searching for hidden literary treasure.
Though the collection is divided into
genres, don't expect much else in the
way of organization in the organically
developed stacks.

Haebangchon 해방촌

Haebangchon is a mixed space
of residential alleys, older expat-
oriented restaurants and pubs, newer
establishments catering to the young
and social media savvy, independent
bookstores and art spaces, all in the
shadow of the iconic N Seoul Tower.

Fat Cat is a neighborhood bistro
and brunch place that's been around
in one form or another forever. Another
local institution is the expat sports
pub Phillies. Casablanca does some
mean Moroccan sandwiches. For lovely
desserts in sophisticated surroundings,
try the café The Hackney. Community
space Pocket uses upcycled objects in

> "Gyeongnidan-gil is a small town and everyone knows each other. It's a really close community, almost like a family."
>
> —Charlie Kim, Berkeley Coffee Social

its effort to be Seoul's first sustainable bar. **Laundry Project** is both a café and a coin-op laundry. The cozy roastery and café **Le Café** is a beloved local fixture. For something more literary, browse the wide selection of independent magazines and books at **Storage Books and Film** ②.

Not to be missed is the **Sinheung Market** ③, at the top of the hill. Young merchants are transforming this old neighborhood market into a vibrant center of commerce and creativity. The café **OrangOrang** helped start it all—check out the view from the rooftop space.

HBC's artist community holds several festivals throughout the year, including the HBC Festival, a biannual live music festival.

Huam-dong 후암동

Just beyond Haebangchon, in a valley on the slope of Namsan Mountain, is the neighborhood of Huam-dong. Interesting things are starting to happen

here, too, albeit at a much slower pace than Gyeongnidan and Haebangchon. The burger joint **The 100 Food Truck** ① (not actually a food truck) and the café/bar **Oriole** offer panoramic views of the cityscape from their rooftop terraces. Overlooking the rotary near Yongsan Middle School is **Sowolgil Milyeong**, a quaint bakery café that doubles as a local salon. **Mid Century Mood Coffee** brings a heavy dose of sophistication, and its wave toast is an Instagram favorite. **Anarchy Bros** turns a historical colonial-era home into a cool café/bar.

Seongsu-dong 성수동

 Seongsu, Line 2

The "Brooklyn of Seoul," Seongsu-dong blends the industrial and the chic to create one of the city's hippest destinations. This gritty old neighborhood of factories and warehouses on the bank of the Hangang River hosts an ever-growing number of trendy cafés, restaurants, bars, galleries and boutiques, many in renovated industrial properties. The bohemian and blue-collar live and work side-by-side here, feeding off one another's know-how, energy and creativity, the streets dancing to the tune of machinery, indie music and the rumble of the subway passing overhead on the elevated tracks. The street art everywhere reinforces the vibe.

Historically, Seongsu-dong has been the center of Korea's handmade shoe industry, too. Many cordwainers ply their trade here still, both old pros who have been at it for decades and young artisans with dreams of becoming the next Jimmy Choo.

If you need a break from the urban, you can always pop into nearby Seoul Forest, the city's answer to New York's Central Park.

Yeonmujang-gil 연무장길

Probably better known as "the area with a lot of hot cafés," this old industrial area — and before that, a military training ground during the Joseon era — has some of the trendiest, most Instaready cafés in Seoul, including, but by no means limited to, **Daelim Changgo**, **Onion**, **or.er.**, **Urban Source** and **Zagmachi**. Mixed in with the factories and cafés are stylishly urban select shops, offering a curated assortment of brands. Such places include **SUPY**, **Velvet Trunk** and **WxDxH**. Finish exploring the area with a pint at local brew pub **Amazing Brewery**.

Daelim Changgo 대림창고 ①

One of Seongsu-dong's pioneers, Daelim Changgo was a rice mill and warehouse before becoming one of Seoul's hippest spots. The brick walls of this cavernous industrial space house

a café, restaurant, bar and exhibit space with some impressive works of installation art. The place hosts fashion shows, editorial shoots, parties and other events, too. Somewhere this cool can get a bit crowded, however, and you'll need to pay a KRW 10,000 entrance fee on the weekend—it comes with one free drink.

S–Factory ②

Another industrial site was transformed into an arts and commerce complex that includes exhibition spaces, shops, ateliers, restaurants and cafés. It has hosted some major shows, including a digital art exhibition dedicated to the work of Austrian painter Gustav Klimt and an exhibit of work by British photographer Patty Boyd, the muse of George Harrison and Eric Clapton.

Common Ground and Under Stand Avenue

Twenty-somethings flock to **Common Ground** ③④, a shopping center and cultural space composed of 200 blue shipping containers near Konkuk University. Here you'll find lifestyle brands both international and Korean, curated collections of works by young local designers, popular restaurants

> "Seongsu-dong is a neighborhood where Seoul Forest, red brick factories built in the 1970s and modern high-rises coexist. Factories, manufacturers and handmade shoe artisans operate in Seongsu-dong, but so do designers. Various designers—including those who work in leather, printing, shoes, architecture, photography and fashion—are collaborating with the artisans who work here."
>
> —Kim Jae-won, or.er.

and cafés and a handful of food trucks. The space hosts plenty of art shows, concerts and promotional events, too. It's a really happening place.

Since just one cultural space composed of shipping containers is never enough, we also present to you **Under Stand Avenue** ⑤, composed of 116 container boxes near the entrance of Seoul Forest. This cooperative project between private, public and non-profit entities has open arts spaces and shops for environmentally friendly and socially conscience brands in additional to the obligatory places to eat and drink. And it looks pretty.

Yeonnam-dong 연남동

 Hongik Univ., Line 2, Gyeongui-Jungang, Airport Railroad

Not so long ago, Yeonnam-dong was a quiet residential district of narrow alleyways lined by low-rise homes. A couple of years ago, however, young artists, chefs and other creative types—many fleeing gentrifying neighborhoods like Hongdae—began settling in the area, opening small, highly personal shops. Many more soon followed. Before long, the quiet residential neighborhood had become Seoul's "it" place, the city's little piece of hipster heaven.

To be sure, many people still actually live in Yeonnam-dong. But they've been joined by stylish cafés, modish boutiques, quaint guest houses, independent bookstores, art markets and some of the finest choices of international eats in the country. The recent opening of Gyeongui Line Forest Park, a disused railway line-turned-urban green space, has accelerated the neighborhood's development still more. On a weekend, it can seem every young couple with a smart phone and an Instagram account is there, but don't let that put you off—you'll still find plenty of space to relax and be you.

Dongjin Market 동진시장 ❸

In their competition with supermarkets and other large distributors, traditional markets have fared poorly. Yeonnam-dong's Dongjin Market was no exception. Mostly abandoned, the market seemed ready for the dustbin of history when young artists took it over, using the old covered arcade for regular arts and crafts markets. They currently host flea markets on Friday night and Saturday and Sunday afternoon. The musty old market with its vintage signs offers a charming contrast with the youthful creativity taking place under its roof.

The market has also rejuvenated the surrounding alleyways. In the immediate vicinity of the market are one of Seoul's most highly regarded coffee houses (**Coffee Libre**, p. 143), a very good Mexican restaurant (**B'Mucho** ⑥), a Vietnamese sandwich shop (**Lai Lai Lai** ④), a charming tea shop (**Salon De Ceylon** ①), a handmade sourdough bagel shop (**San Francisco Bagels**), a Japanese curry house (**Himeji** ②) and a branch of the popular Thai noodle shop **Tuk Tuk Noodles**, a Yeonnam-dong institution. And that's just scratching the surface.

Gyeongui Line Forest Park 경의선숲길공원

Beginning operation in 1905, the old Gyeongui Line used to link Seoul with Sinuiju, a northern city on what is now

the border between North Korea and China. Since the Korean War, however, trains have run only as far the DMZ. In 1999, work began turning the old line into an electrified commuter line to service Seoul's northern suburbs. In Seoul, the line—previously above ground—was turned into a subway.

The narrow, 6.3 kilometer-long strip of land running along the disused railway was turned into a green space called Gyeongui Line Forest Park. The Yeonnam-dong section, which opened in 2015, is the longest and most popular stretch. The grassy, tree-lined park, flanked by two endless lines of cafés and eateries, draws so many visitors that it's earned the nickname "Yeontral Park." In summer, it can seem like one giant picnic, especially at night, when friends, families and lovers break out the picnic mats for an evening of good food and frosty beverages.

Little Chinatown

Thanks to the nearby Chinese middle and high school, many *hwagyo*—ethnic Chinese residents of Korea—live in the Yeonnam-dong area. The local dining scene reflects this, naturally. You'll find several dozen Chinese restaurants in Yeonnam-dong, including about 10 that have been around for decades such as **Hyangmi** ⑤, **Ha Ha** and **Ipumbunsik**. In addition to usual Sino-Korean staples such as *jjajangmyeon*, *jjamppong* and *tangsuyuk*, these places also serve dishes such as fried shrimp sandwiches, fried eggplant in a sweet and sour sauce and Chinese-style chilled noodles served with peanut sauce. Nowadays, places specializing in Taiwanese street food are popping up, too—give **Little Taiwan** or **Daeman Yasijang** a try.

> "To me, Yeonnam-dong is like a treasure hunt. It's a fun treasure island of many kinds of people, many kinds of shops, many kinds of expressions."
>
> —You Byeong-seok, Little Press Coffee

Mangwon-dong 망원동

Mangwon, Line 6

Not far from Yeonnam-dong, Mangwon-dong was little more than a quiet, working-class residential district with a history of flooding. Now it's the area's newest "it" place, one that, at least for now, retains a connection with its former self. Unlike some of the city's more gentrified hot spots, Mangwon-dong is still a living, breathing neighborhood of peaceful residential streets, bustling traditional markets and elderly denizens chatting in front of the local grocery store.

When you're done exploring the alleys and markets, visit the Mangwon section of Hangang Park, perhaps in time to watch the sun set over the river. You can also learn a bit about Korean naval history—and have a bit of fun at the same time—at Seoul Battleship Park.

Poeun-ro (a.k.a. Mangnidan-gil) 포은로(망리단길)

Mangwon-dong's hipsterland stretches from Mangwon Station to the alleyways surrounding Mangwon Market, with much activity focused on Poeun-ro, a 500-meter stretch of colorful and highly individualistic places to eat, drink and make merry, most little more than hole-in-the-walls with simple menus. Many call the area "Mangnidan-gil," referring to the similarly hip area of Gyeongnidan-gil,

though this is frowned upon by the locals worried about gentrification.

Though **Coffee Gage Donggyeong** is located in a basement and has no sign, there are almost always waiting lists full of people come to try their Vienna coffee and enjoy the ambiance. The charmingly rustic **Joo5il Sikdang's** ① simple menu includes butter chicken curry, chicken shrimp gumbo and

"I came to Mangwon-dong in 2015. At that time, Mangwon-dong really felt like a place where people lived. A tree-lined street was out in front, the Hangang River was nearby . . . it was a neighborhood where it seemed you could live a leisurely life. I raise two dogs, and it was a good place to walk them."

—Kim Dongkeun, Le Glacier des Étoiles

shakshuka. At night, **Bokdeokbang** serves home-style Korean cooking and *makgeolli* sourced from throughout the country. The adorable **Le Glacier des Étoiles** ③ serves French home cooking, but is better known for its ice cream. The café **Zapangi** ②, which means "vending machine," is a local icon for its door, which looks like a pink vending machine.

There are plenty of boutiques and shops, too, including the Japanese-style vintage shop **Subaco** and the pleasant little bookstore **Uhjjuhdah Bookshop**.

Mangwon Market 망원시장

Born in 1975, Mangwon Market grew even more vibrant after it was modernized in 2008. The influx of younger merchants and shoppers hasn't hurt, either. For visitors, the market is a great place to fill up on the cheap. The specialties include fried chicken bits, or *dak-gangjeong*; handmade croquettes; hand-cut noodles, or *kalguksu*; and fresh fruit, which you can buy cheaper here than in most other places in Seoul.

Zero Space 제로 스페이스

Zero Space is the offline showroom of Zero To Zero (www.zeroperzero. com), an innovative graphic studio best known overseas for their series of city subway maps that integrate local symbols into their design. Their world map is pretty cool, too. At their shop, you can find the studio's full selection of maps, books, posters, cards, travel accessories and more.

Hangang Park and Seoul Battleship Park 한강공원과 서울함공원

As Mangwon-dong sits along the Hangang River, it boasts a section of Hangang Park, complete with grass

fields for picnics, tennis courts and other sports facilities and, of course, views of the river. The park is a great place to take in the sunset, too. If you'd like to make a picnic out of it, there are a bunch of chicken joints near the entrance of the park that will be happy to help.

The newest addition to the park is Seoul Battleship Park, where three museum ships are on display. The largest is the Frigate Seoul, a 1,900-ton frigate decommissioned in 2015. There's also a midget submarine you can explore, too. Kids will love the place.

Historic Architecture

Though long maligned by many as little more than a giant sea of concrete apartments, Seoul possesses a rich architectural heritage. Though it's undoubtedly true that many historic buildings were lost during the colonial era, Korean War and the post-war industrialization, much still survives, albeit often hidden in the urban sprawl.

Seoul was the royal capital of Joseon Dyansty (1392–1910) for five centuries. Unsurprisingly, therefore, many of the city's heritage buildings date from this period. Joseon's contributions include five royal palaces, several major Confucian shrines and the old stone walls that circle the old city. Colonial Japan, too, left its mark, erecting symbols of imperial prestige and authority such as Seoul's old central train station and the darkly imposing Seodaemun Prison. Western missionaries added grand cathedrals and churches to the cityscape. Even during the colonial era, Koreans were busy building, too, creating sprawling neighborhoods of Korean-style *hanok* homes, including the now iconic Bukchon Hanok Village.

Changdeokgung Palace 창덕궁

Though the landmark Gyeongbokgung Palace may be bigger, the Changdeokgung Palace is the most beautiful of Seoul's five historical royal palaces, a jewel of Joseon Dynasty architecture and the pinnacle of Korean gardening. No visit to Seoul would be complete without a stroll through the palace's stunning Huwon Garden, a masterfully crafted landscape of forested hills, flowers, ponds and pleasure pavilions where the kings and queens of old found inspiration and solace.

Changdeokgung is the second oldest of palaces, first built in the early 15th century and rebuilt in the early 17th century. In contrast to Gyeongbokgung, whose main structures are carefully aligned along a central axis, the placement of Changdeokgung Palace's halls, gates and courtyards is more free-flowing, the hilly terrain determining the layout, a beautiful illustration of one of traditional Korean architecture's defining principles—respect for nature.

The Huwon Garden encompasses over 340,000 square meters of richly forested hillside. Like English gardens, the Huwon Garden presents an idealized vision of nature, its human touches aiming to accentuate, not dominate. Particularly beautiful is the Buyongji Pond, a square, pavilion-lined pond with a round, tree-covered island. The pond expresses the traditional concept of the cosmos, in which the heavens were round and the earth square.

📍 99, Yulgok-ro, Jongno-gu

📞 02-3668-2300

💰 KRW 3,000 (minus the Huwon Garden). KRW 8,000 (for the palace and the Huwon Garden). You must join a guided tour to enter the Huwon Garden—see the website for times.

🌐 eng.cdg.go.kr

Jongmyo Shrine 종묘

Jongmyo Shrine is a masterpiece of Joseon architecture, one deeply informed by the Confucian ethics upon which the kingdom was built. The shrine hosted the memorial ceremonies for the kings and queens of Joseon, one of the most important rites performed by the royal court. The largest hall, the Jeongjeon, houses 49 spirit tablets of Joseon's 19 kings and 30 queens, including that of King Taejo, the founder of Joseon. Some 101 meters long, it is one of the longest wooden structures in East Asia.

The long, low-slung main halls are one with the thick forests that surround the shrine and the mountains beyond. Unlike the brightly painted buildings of the palaces, Jongmyo's halls are more reserved, more somber, a reflection of Confucian modesty, simplicity and frugality.

The Jeonju Yi clan, the royal family of Joseon, performs the old royal memorial ceremony at Jongmyo on the first Sunday of May. The ceremony and its music and dance were added to UNESCO's list of Masterpieces of the Oral and Intangible Heritage of Humanity in 2001.

- 157, Jong-ro, Jongno-gu
- 02-765-0195
- KRW 1,000
- english.cha.go.kr

Munmyo Confucian Shrine and Seonggyungwan National Academy

문묘와 성균관

One of Seoul's best kept secrets is hidden away in a corner of Sungkyunkwan University in Daehangno.

Munmyo Confucian Shrine houses memorial tablets for Confucius and for venerated Confucian scholars from Korea and China. Though the original shrine was completed in 1398, what you see now dates from a 17th century reconstruction. The tablets are kept in the grand main hall, the Daeseongjeon, and the two halls that flank the central courtyard.

A stone path, reserved for the spirits of those enshrined here, leads from the Daeseongjeon to the southern gate, where the spirits enter. This gate is opened only on important occasions such as memorial rites.

Just next to the shrine is another courtyard with an old lecture hall flanked by two long rows of dormitories. This is what remains of the historical Seonggyungwan National Academy, Joseon's highest center of Confucian learning. The dormitory halls, built in the 17th century, are simple, unpretentious and utterly charming. A pair of 600-year-old ginkgo trees grow in the courtyard. The ginkgo enjoys a long association with Confucianism as Confucius enjoyed reading and teaching his students under a ginkgo tree in his home town.

📍 31, Seonggyungwan-ro, Jongno-gu
📞 02-760-1472
Ⓦ Free
🌐 www.skk.or.kr

Unhyeongung Palace 운현궁

Although the *gung* in its name means "palace," Unhyeongung Palace was not a palace in the strictest sense. Nevertheless, the beautiful 19th century mansion was the center of power in Joseon for 10 years beginning in 1864, when it was the home of Heungseon Daewongun, the powerful prince regent and father of King Gojong, who also lived here until he came of age in 1874. During this decade, the estate grew so large that it rivaled the royal palaces in scale.

Though considerably smaller than it was at its height, Unhyeongung Palace remains one of the most spectacular Joseon-era homes in the country. The residence is comprised of several wooden halls, courtyards, walls and gardens. Unlike the official palaces, which are colorfully painted, the residence's wooden structures are unpainted, lending the home a genteel, rustic beauty. Particularly eye-catching is the Irodang Hall, with its lovely inner garden visible through the hall's sliding wood-and-paper doors.

Just next door to Unhyeongung Palace is the Unhyeongung Yanggwan, a Baroque two-story mansion built in 1912 as a home for Heungseon Daewongun's grandson.

> 📍 464, Samil-daero, Jongno-gu
> 📞 02-766-9090
> Ⓦ Free
> 🌐 www.unhyeongung.or.kr

Bukchon Hanok Village 북촌한옥마을

One of Seoul's most popular destinations, Bukchon Hanok Village covers the low hills between Gyeongbokgung Palace in the west and Changdeokgung Palace in the east. In the days of Joseon, wealthy aristocratic scholars and officials maintained large estates in the area, which was prized for its fine views of Namsan Mountain, excellent drainage and auspicious feng shui. In the 1920s and 1930s, however, the large estates were carved up into smaller divisions, upon which were built tile roof homes, or *hanok*, many of which survive today. The neighborhood boasts over 600 such homes, the largest collection in Seoul.

Bukchon's *hanok* homes differ from "traditional" homes of the Joseon era. Customized for the urban environment, the homes are lined up one next to the other, townhouse style, and optimized for space with shorter eaves and other elements. They also incorporate modernities such as glass windows and galvanized metal gutters, reflecting the neighborhood's early 20th century origins.

One of the more spectacular homes in the area is the Baek In-je House, a palatial estate from 1913 that incorporates influences from abroad, including Japanese-style wooden corridors linking the men's and women's chambers.

> ♀ 37, Gyedong-gil, Jongno-gu
> ☎ 02-2133-1372
> ⊕ bukchon.seoul.go.kr

Culture Station Seoul 284 문화역서울 284

Completed in 1925, the former Seoul Station was one of the Japanese colonial regime's most prominent showpieces, the second largest train station in East Asia behind Tokyo Station when it opened. The striking structure of red brick and granite is still a site to see, with its Renaissance symmetry, Baroque details, Byzantine domed roof and Jazz Age interior finishings. Until 2004, when it closed upon the opening of the new Seoul Station next door, the grand edifice was Korea's most important railway hub. During Korea's post-war development years, the station welcomed countless people migrating to Seoul from the countryside in search of jobs and other opportunities.

Disused for several years after its closing, the old Seoul Station was restored, renamed and reopened in 2011 as an art space called Culture Station Seoul 284. The venue hosts exhibits, shows, performances and lectures throughout the year.

- 📍 1, Tongil-ro, Jung-gu
- 📞 02-3407-3500
- ⓦ Admission depends on programs.
- 🌐 www.seoul284.org

Seodaemun Prison History Hall 서대문형무소역사관

In 1908, the Korean royal government—by then dominated by Imperial Japan—built Korea's first modern prison outside Seodaemun Gate, Seoul's western entrance. Japan made its control of Korea official in 1910 when it forcefully annexed the country, and soon enough, the prison was filled with independence activists, political prisoners and whoever else may have incurred the colonial authorities' wrath. At one point, following the nationwide independence demonstrations of March 1, 1919, the colonial regime incarcerated over 3,000 Korean protesters in the prison, including the iconic Yu Gwan-sun, a student at a girl's high school who died at Seodaemun after she was imprisoned for leading a pro-independence demonstration.

Even after Korea regained its independence in 1945, the authorities continued to find use for Seodaemun Prison, locking away behind its walls democracy activists, leftists and other dissidents. With the opening of a new prison just outside of Seoul in 1987, Seodaemun Prison was turned into a historical park.

Like many old prisons in world, Seodaemun Prison is ironically beautiful—it is, after all, a castle of sorts, and its weathered brick walls have a timeless grace.

> 📍 251, Tongil-ro, Seodaemun-gu
> 📞 02-360-8590
> 💲 KRW 3,000
> 🌐 www.facebook.com/sdmprison

Seoul Cathedral Anglican Church of Korea

대한성공회 서울주교좌성당

Located near the British embassy in Jeong-dong, Seoul's old legation quarter, Seoul Cathedral Anglican Church of Korea is one of the finest works of Romanesque Revival in East Asia. Though British architect Arthur Stansfield Dixon's design called for a grand cathedral in the shape of the Latin cross, the church was only half-completed when it was consecrated in 1926. In the 1990s, however, the church was expanded after a museum employee rediscovered the original blueprint in a British library.

With its thick walls, round arches and blind arcading, the cathedral typifies the Romanesque Revival of the 19th and 20th centuries. Dixon managed to sneak in some Korean elements, too, such as the wooden frames of the clerestory windows. George Jack, a Scottish artist active in the British Arts and Crafts Movement of the early 20th century, designed the beautiful gold mosaics behind the altar.

Behind the church is the rectory, built in the early 20th century in a fusion of Korean and Western styles, and the Yangijae Hall, a Korean-style wooden hall that used to be part of Deoksugung Palace and is now used by the Anglican Church as an office.

> 📍 15, Sejong-daero 21-gil, Jung-gu
> 📞 02-730-6611

Yongsan Seminary and the Chapel of the Sacred Heart of Jesus 서울용산신학교와 원효로 예수성심성당

Hidden on the campus of Sacred Heart Girls High School in Yongsan, Yongsan Seminary and the Chapel of the Sacred Heart of Jesus are underappreciated architectural gems from the turn of the 20th century.

Korea's first Catholic seminary, Yongsan Seminary moved from Gyeonggi-do to its current location on a hill overlooking the Hangang River in 1887. A new Western-style schoolhouse was completed in 1892. The simple two-story building with big arched windows is now used as an office by the nuns of the Society of the Sacred Heart of Jesus.

Even more stunning is the Chapel of the Sacred Heart of Jesus, the seminary's old sanctuary. Though small, it is beautiful and well preserved. Completed in 1902, the church sits on a steep slope with three floors on the downhill side and two on the uphill one. Like many historical Catholic churches in Korea, the chapel is built of red and gray bricks and embraces an eclectic style mixing Gothic and Romanesque elements. The interior, with its simple vaulted ceiling, pointed Gothic windows and stained glass behind the altar, is especially atmospheric.

> 📍 49, Wonhyo-ro 19-gil, Yongsan-gu
> 📞 02-701-5501

Seoul City Wall 서울한양도성

First erected in 1396, Seoul's historical city walls were more than just defensive bulwarks to protect the city from attack. The walls defined the royal capital's limits, regulated commerce and trade and kept the city's population steady. Over six centuries after they were built, the walls continue to play a defensive role, with sections patrolled by soldiers or police.

Built by over 200,000 conscripted laborers, the walls snake 18 kilometers along the ridges of the mountains that guard Seoul's old downtown. In the old days, four grand gates controlled passage through the walls; three still remain, including the iconic Sungnyemun (Namdaemun) and Heunginjimun (Dongdaemun) gates. Modern history was unkind to the walls, with the Japanese colonial regime demolishing segments to build roads and the Korean War destroying or damaging what was left. Work to restore what was lost, begun in 1968, continues to this day.

Hiking trails take you along the entirety of the wall. The trail along Bugaksan Mountain boasts the most original segments of wall, while the trails along Inwangsan, Naksan and Namsan mountains have the best views.

⊕ seoulcitywall.seoul.go.kr

The Other Side of Bukchon

Bukchon is one of the hottest tourist attractions in Seoul. Every day, thousands of people from all over the world swamp its narrow alleys, taking selfies against the backdrop of the *hanok* homes that dominate the inner parts of this historic area. The Internet and guidebooks usually say—or at least want you to believe—that this is where the *yangban*, the pre-modern Korean aristocrats, used to live. Hence Bukchon's nickname: the *yangban* village of Seoul. Located on a gentle southern slope with good drainage, full exposure to the sunlight, great views of the city center and proximity to two main palaces, Bukchon seems like the perfect place for the most privileged of old Korea.

History tells us that this is only half-true, however. Most large *yangban* residences, once common in the lower parts of Bukchon, are all but gone. The oldest of the remaining few, the Yun Residence, was built as late as 1870. The higher parts of Bukchon had fewer homes in the old days. Koreans were valley dwellers by tradition and necessity. Rarely, if at all, did Koreans inhabit high terrain, where water was scarce. Photos from the late Joseon period reveal utterly barren hills behind Gyeongbokgung Palace, confirming this.

Then what about the rows of tiled-roof houses on top of those hills now?

They are the product of a massive urban influx and building boom in the 1930s, fully two decades after Joseon and its social class system—including the *yangban*—ceased to exist. Enter Jeong Segwon, a maverick developer. His real estate company, Geonyangsa, was the key player in turning most of the barren hills of Bukchon into the cradle of modern *hanok* we see today. He and other savvy developers introduced modernized planning, mass production, elements of standardization and even modern financing for the consumers. That all this happened while Korea was ruled by Japan is even more remarkable.

This side of the story is seldom mentioned in the promotional literature about Bukchon, not because it is false, but because this isn't the story the authorities want tourists to believe. Some tourist pamphlets or museum explanations are written so ambiguously that even though they never outright lie, they invite you to believe that the *hanok* you see in Bukchon were indeed where *yangban* used to live. People like Jeong Segwon are conveniently ignored for a more attractive version of manufactured history.

But isn't it more thrilling, at least from a contemporary point of view, that what seems like an old village is in fact a modern creation? Jeong Segwon was not just a businessman—he was also a patriot who contributed much money to Korea's independence movement. Isn't this story of greater value for the democratic republic Korea is now? What's the point of covering it up for a historical fairy tale? If your Bukchon guidebook does not mention people like Jeong Segwon, throw it away—you are missing the other and more exciting truth about the neighborhood.

Written by Hwang Doojin

Hwang Doojin founded Seoul-based architectural firm Doojin Hwang Architects (djharch.com) in 2000. He has taken a keen interest in urban regeneration, especially in the Bukchon area, where he has overseen the restoration and modernization of several historical *hanok* homes.

Arts & Culture

Though places such as the War Memorial of Korea and National Museum of Korea are obvious destinations for tourists visiting Seoul, the city boasts many lesser-known cultural spaces worth visiting. Often preferred by Seoulites themselves, these contemporary art spaces and off-the-beaten-track museums present in-depth perspectives into local preferences rather than broad overviews of Korean culture.

Yun Hyong-keun Retrospective

Works by siren eun young jung

Yun Hyong-keun Retrospective

National Museum of Modern and Contemporary Art, Korea (MMCA) 국립현대미술관

The MMCA's flagship museum, MMCA Seoul, is located next to Gyeongbokgung Palace. With eight galleries, a digital library and rotating outdoor exhibitions, the museum provides a comprehensive experience for the contemporary art lover. The beautiful space, designed by local architect Mihn Hyunjun, incorporates architecture from three periods: a historical government building from the Joseon era, an old hospital from the Japanese colonial era, and a stylish modern wing designed by Mihn himself. Set aside at least several hours to explore the place properly. One highlight is the Young Architects Program, held every summer, when the museum erects a temporary outdoor installation to provide shade and comfort to passersby.

The MMCA operates two other spaces in and around Seoul. The MMCA Deoksugung, on the grounds of historical Deoksugung Palace, hosts exhibits modern art both from Korea and from around the world. The MMCA Gwacheon, located in the southern suburb of Gwacheon, boasts a collection that includes *Dadaikseon*, a six-story tower of 1,003 television sets created by the late video artist Nam June Paik.

MMCA Seoul	MMCA Deoksugung
📍 30, Samcheong-ro, Jongno-gu	📍 99, Sejong-daero, Jung-gu
📞 02-3701-9500	📞 02-2188-0600
🅦 KRW 4,000	🅦 Admission depends on programs.
🌐 www.mmca.go.kr	

The exhibition *Voiceless: Return of the Foreclosed* © Seoul Museum of Art

Seoul Museum of Art (SeMA) 서울시립미술관

SeMA's flagship space is a three-story building just behind Deoksugung Palace, at the end of the promenade along the palace's outer stone wall. Erected in 1928, the building was previously a courthouse; its historical Renaissance-style façade was preserved when the space was renovated to host the museum, which relocated here in 2002. The museum boats about 4,700 works of modern and contemporary art, including over 90 works by the renowned 20th century painter Chun Kyung-ja. It also hosts two international exhibitions a year. These shows, which often mix art and pop culture, have included an exhibition of work by K-pop star G-Dragon, a DreamWorks exhibition sponsored by GNC Media and a Hyundai Card project dedicated to filmmaker Stanley Kubrick. As these special exhibits can get quite popular, expect long lines on weekends.

SeMA operates several other spaces around the city, including the Nam-Seoul Museum of Art in Gwanak and the Buk-Seoul Museum in Nowon.

- 61, Deoksugung-gil, Jung-gu
- 02-2124-8800
- Free except for special exhibitions.
- sema.seoul.go.kr

Everything is Inside, Subodh Gupta, 2004

First Impressions, Yoon Hyangro, 2014

(From left to right) *Untitled*, CI Kim, 2013. *Dream*, CI Kim, 2016.
Warhol in Astonishment, Hyung Koo Kang, 2010

ARARIO MUSEUM in SPACE 아라리오 뮤지엄 인 스페이스

The ARARIO's story begins with Kim Chang-il, the founder of the family of contemporary art museums. One of the world's top art collectors, Kim is a self-made millionaire who fell in love with art while traveling abroad. Opening up his first gallery in 1989, he now runs several spaces in Korea and one in Shanghai.

In 2014, he opened his private collection to the public in the iconic former headquarters of the SPACE Group, the architecture firm founded by the late Kim Swoo-geun, one of the country's greatest 20th century architects. Overlooking Changdeokgung Palace, the museum houses works by Nam June Paik, Andy Warhol, Cindy Sherman and Keith Haring, among others.

When you're finished looking at the art, avail yourself on some of the space's excellent dining options, including its much-lauded café and bakery and the fifth floor Dining in Space, a French restaurant that earned a Michelin star in 2017.

- 📍 83, Yulgok-ro, Jongno-gu
- 📞 02-736-5700
- 💲 KRW 10,000
- 🌐 www.arariomuseum.org

Multi-media exhibition *Weather* at D-Museum

Weather

Weather

Daelim Museum 대림미술관

The Daelim Group, a local conglomerate, operates three popular museums: the Daelim Museum, the D-Museum and D Project Space. Located in the pleasant Seochon area west of Gyeongbokgung Palace, the Daelim Museum initially focused on photography when it was founded in 1997, but it has since broadened its scope to include all aspects of design, calling itself "the museum where everyday turns into art." Since opening in the hip Hannam-dong neighborhood in 2015, the D-Museum has developed into one of the city's trendiest art spaces, and certainly one of its most Instagrammed. Focusing on design and modern art with an interactive twist, the museum has earned praise—and sometimes criticism—for its easily digestible content. Alternatively, the D Project Space, a renovated former billiards hall down the street from the D-Museum, is a smaller venue that shows lesser-known, more obscure works. While you can expect crowds at the Daelim Museum and the D-Museum on weekends, the D Project Space is likely free—both in terms of space and cost.

Daelim Museum	D-Museum	D Project Space
📍 21, Jahamun-ro 4-gil, Jongno-gu	📍 5-6, Dokseodang-ro 29-gil, Yongsan-gu	📍 B3, 85, Dokseodang-ro, Yongsan-gu
📞 02-720-0667	📞 070-5097-0020	📞 02-3785-0667
💰 KRW 8,000	💰 KRW 9,000	💰 Free
🌐 www.daelimmuseum.org		

Dongdaemun Design Plaza (DDP) 동대문디자인플라자

Likened to a UFO that has crash-landed in the heart of Seoul, the futuristic DDP is one of the city's most iconic structures. Designed by the late British architect Zaha Hadid, the first woman to win the Pritzker Prize, the undulating mass of concrete, aluminum and steel has helped put Seoul on the international architecture map, often appearing in international magazines. The building has had its detractors, too, high among them being Seoul Mayor Park Won-soon, who not only called it "ugly," but did so during its opening ceremony.

Currently operated by the Seoul Design Foundation, the DDP has exhibition spaces, design shops, workshops, cafés and more. It hosts a never-ending calendar of arts and design-related exhibitions and shows, including Seoul Fashion Week, Korea's biggest celebration of fashion, held in spring and autumn. It's also the temporary home of the Kansong Art Museum, one of the world's best collections of traditional Korean art.

One of the DDP's highlights is the popular LED Rose Garden, an outdoor field of 25,550 LED roses, lit from 7 p.m. to midnight as a celebration of seven decades of independence from imperial rule.

📍 281, Eulji-ro, Jung-gu
📞 02-2153-0408
🌐 www.ddp.or.kr

Piknic 피크닉

Opened only in May of 2018, this new five-story culture center run by design studio Glint quickly got the attention of Seoul's trendsetters. Perched on the lower slopes of Namsan Mountain, Piknic includes exhibition halls, a café, a bar, a restaurant and a rooftop space with panoramic views of the mountain and the cityscape below.

Piknic's first exhibition, *LIFE, L I F E*, added visual and sensory elements to the work of Japanese musician Ryuichi Sakamoto, demonstrating Glint's well-deserved reputation for turning art into an immersive experience. You can also enjoy Kafe Piknic on the first floor and the modern European restaurant Zero Complex (see p. 103) on the third floor. Pick up a souvenir from KioskKiosk, a lifestyle store that sells stationary products and home goods.

- 30, Toegye-ro 6ga-gil, Jung-gu
- 02-6245-6371
- www.piknic.kr

Yoon Dong-ju Literary House 윤동주문학관

The revered Korean poet Yoon Dong-ju lived in a boarding house at the foot of Inwangsan Mountain in the 1940s. Perhaps inspired by his walks on the mountain, Yoon wrote beloved poems such as "A Night for Counting Stars" and "Self-portrait." To commemorate Yoon, Jongno-gu opened a museum for the poet in 2012. Architect Lee Sojin renovated a disused water pumping station on the slope of Inwangsan, transforming it into an emotionally moving space.

The museum has three galleries. The first exhibits Yoon's personal items and showcases his work. The second, an old water tank opened to the sky, symbolizes the water well discussed in "Self-portrait." The third, also a disused water tank, is closed and dark. This space, used as a mediation room and a theater showing a short film about Yoon, recalls the Japanese prison cell in which the young poet died.

A walk on the nearby Poet's Hill provides great views of Seoul on a clear day, but the intensity of the indoor spaces are better felt in the gray and rain. The Cheongun Literature Library, a lovely *hanok* library located just up the hill from the Yoon Dong-ju Literary House, is also worth a visit.

> 📍 119, Changuimun-ro, Jongno-gu
> 📞 02-2148-4175
> 💲 Free

Cheongun Literature Library

Korea Furniture Museum 한국가구박물관

Praised by CNN as the most beautiful museum in Seoul, the Korea Furniture Museum is a reservation-only exhibit space in Seongbuk-dong. Unofficially open since 2008, the impressive museum has ten *hanok* and 2,000 pieces of furniture with pieces that date back to the Joseon era. In recent years, it has also hosted important events, including a special luncheon for the 2010 Seoul G20 Summit, a concert by pianist Lang Lang and a luncheon for Chinese President Xi Jinping during a state visit to Korea in 2014. That politicians are frequent visitors should come as no surprise since the museum's founder, the renowned furniture collector Chyung Mi-sook, is the daughter of Lee Tai-young, Korea's first female lawyer, and many members of her family have served as lawmakers in the country's parliament. Tours run about an hour and are available in English, Chinese, Japanese and Korean. Though photography is restricted to certain areas only, the museum is well worth the extra planning involved to visit.

📍 121, Daesagwan-ro, Seongbuk-gu
📞 02-745-0181
🅦 KRW 20,000
🌐 kofum.com

Oil Tank Culture Park 문화비축기지

Oil Tank Culture Park is a great example of urban regeneration in Seoul. The park consists of six disused tanks once belonging to a high-security petroleum storage facility built in the wake of the 1973 oil crisis. Shut down in 2000, the storage compound underwent an extensive renovation to transform it into a cultural complex. The new space opened in 2017. The park has several performance halls, an exhibition center, an information center and a large, outdoor stage that looks like a Greek amphitheater at the bottom of a deep pit. One of the old tanks has been preserved in its original condition to provide some historical continuity. Even when there are no prominent exhibitions, many visit simply to photograph the unique tangents and arcs of the space. The park hosts a weekend night market in the spring, summer and autumn, too.

- 87, Jeungsan-ro, Mapo-gu
- 02-376-8410
- www.facebook.com/culturetank

Emu Artspace 복합문화공간 에무

Named for the Renaissance scholar Erasmus, Emu Artspace is a small cultural space tucked into a corner of Gwanghwamun. Open in 2010, the space has a movie theater, concert hall, book café and rooftop terrace. Writers and directors often give talks or workshops here, focusing on everything from French films for children to creating art books. Though the cinema sits only about thirty, it screens Korean films with English subtitles, drawing many international residents.

The cinema also shows independent and foreign-language films rarely screened elsewhere in Korea. Visit Emu Artspace's Facebook page to see the schedule. The space's cozy vibe and panoramic rooftop views have made it a popular date place, too.

📍 7, Gyeonghuigung 1ga-gi, Jongno-gu
📞 02-730-5515
🌐 www.emuartspace.com

Hyundai Card Libraries 현대카드 라이브러리

Hyundai Card, one of Korea's leading credit card companies, has opened four "libraries" that are open to cardholding members only. Offering more than just books, these spaces, featuring collections curated by the world's leading experts, bring together architecture, design and the arts like few other spaces in the city.

The Design Library in Bukchon Hanok Village boasts around 17,000 titles on all things design, from the Bauhaus to today. The Travel Library in Cheongdam-dong has a bottomless collection of travel guides, travelogues and photo books to inspire armchair travelers everywhere. The Cooking Library in Apgujeong-dong, meanwhile, has not only cookbooks, but also cooking spaces and a deli.

The most talked about space by far, however, is the Hyundai Card Music Library in Hannam-dong. Designed by architect Choi Moon-gyu and curated by DJ Soulscape, the library houses 10,000 vinyl records, 3,000 music publications and nine turntables for in-house use. Visitors can browse a collection that ranges from the Kim Sisters to Public Enemy, use a record player for thirty minutes at a time or simply request music from the DJ at hand.

Don't have a Hyundai Card? Then cozy up to someone who does, as Hyundai Card members may bring one guest per visit.

Design Library	Travel Library
📍 31-18, Bukchon-ro, Jongno-gu	📍 18, Seolleung-ro 152-gil, Gangnam-gu
📞 02-3700-2700	📞 02-3485-5509
Music Library	**Cooking Library**
📍 246, Itaewon-ro, Yongsan-gu	📍 46, Apgujeong-ro 46-gil, Gangnam-gu
📞 02-331-6300	📞 02-513-2900
🌐 library.hyundaicard.com	

Korean Indie:

The Next Big Thing?

I was born in Chuncheon, and my family moved to Los Angeles shortly after. It was the 1980s, the pinnacle of American pop music. Kids had no idea who their president was, but they sure knew Michael Jackson. I was obsessed with pop music. I was a sponge, absorbing all. I used to sing every tune I knew and dreamt of becoming a great singer-songwriter like Cyndi Lauper.

After six years, I returned to Korea, where I've lived ever since. Back then, I knew only English-language music. I had no clue about Korean pop music, but after watching cool musicians like Kim Wan-sun on television, I was mesmerized, just as I was by American pop. I learned more about Korean folk and psychedelic music from the 1970s and how it deeply influenced people during the dark times of the military dictatorships. I witnessed the growth of Korean pop music, which had been heavily influenced by American, British and Japanese music.

In May of 2018, something unbelievable happened. A Korean pop group, BTS, topped the Billboard 200 album chart. Had I ever expected that K-pop would be such a global success?

No, I did not.

Though it's hard to explain what "K-pop" is, you could understand the genre as popular Korean music, or "idol" music. After watching overseas "idol" groups like the Spice Girls or 'N Sync or even the Beatles, I believed that without English lyrics, without singers who could pronounce English properly, without songs that simply registered with an English-speaking public, Korean pop music would never make it in the Anglosphere.

I was dead wrong.

With the help of social media, Hallyu, the "Korean Wave," is spreading further and further. We watched Psy go viral, and now, suddenly, Korea is one of the hippest countries in the world. It's not about the language anymore. People the world over can't get enough of our country. How amazing is that?

A humble indie musician, I myself can already feel the hype. Though we may have a long way to go, our band's streaming counts are off the charts. Since the birth of the Korean indie scene in the 1990s, when has Korean indie music ever been so popular overseas? Fans of K-pop, K-dramas or just Korea in general now listen to our music without prejudice, a mind blowing phenomenon.

Korean indie music started at clubs in the Hongik University area—a.k.a Hongdae—in the mid-'90s as a rebellion against mainstream music and media. A bunch of weirdos and misfits began creating new things such as punk rock, modern rock and hip-hop. At the time, the music itself was very Korean. Over time, however, more genres have evolved, and every once in a while, some up-and-coming indie band will overtake the mainstream "idol" groups on the charts when the fresh indie sound and lyrics win over the listening audience.

Korean indie music isn't taking off only in Korea, however. It's growing global, and fast.

As content creators, we should understand that in addition to creating quality content, we must also acknowledge our fans are out there. If we earn more fans worldwide, our industry is going to be just fine. I believe this is the real reason behind K-pop's success.

Whenever I'm interviewed by foreign media, I explain that our target audience might not be here in Korea. Our music never was intended for the Korean market, and anyway, most of our lyrics are in English. Our band is certainly odd that way. We've toured overseas multiple times, and we'll most definitely do so again. If K-pop can conquer the world, why can't K-indie? And if I keep on doing what I believe in, who knows? Might we win a Grammy?

Written by Annie Ko

Launched in 2011 by former skate punk rocker Toby Hwang and fugitive astrophysicist Annie Ko, Love X Stereo is a dazzling Seoul electro rock duo whose dreamy kaleidoscope of stellar synthpop anthems have enraptured music festival audiences across Asia and North America.

lovexstereo.com

Jaha Sonmandu

Dining

Koreans are obsessed about food. Peek over the shoulder of any commuter and chances are they're searching *meokbang* ("eating broadcasting") content to figure out their next meal. Koreans joke that they live to eat, and good food is their reward for a hard day's work. But this love for food is a multifaceted affair. Dining out no longer means communal *hoesik* with one's colleagues: it can mean *honbap* or a special meal just for oneself. And young Koreans are as comfortable doing shots of soju with barbecue as they are washing down pints of craft beer with tacos.

For visitors too, it means a kaleidoscope of dining choices. From decades-old family-run joints to young and hip eateries, there's no lack of choice when it comes to eating out in Seoul. Just remember to bring a big appetite, a fistful of won and you'll leave happy, belly full of great food.

Bongpiyang 봉피양

Bongpiyang describes itself as artisanal *hansik* and barbecue. The franchise also runs Byeokje Galbi, famous for its expensive cuts of premium Korean beef, or *hanu*. At Bongpiyang though, it's about the pork. Their pork ribs are marinated in the house's special sauce that's a little sweet and spicy. The staff expertly grills the ribs at your table, and you can follow up the barbecue with Bongpiyang's famous bowl of Pyongyang *naengmyeon*.

The cold *naengmyeon* broth is savory, and the buckwheat noodles are flavorful and boast great texture. There are instructions on how to enjoy *naengmyeon* on the paper place setting if you're new to it.

If cold noodles aren't your thing however, you can also order Byeokje Galbi's famous *gukbap* or hot stew into which you mix in a bowl of rice. Choose between the rich but mild version or the spicy *yanggomtang* version, filled with tripe and offal.

> 📍 1-4, Yangjae-daero 71-gil, Songpa-gu
> 📞 02-415-5527
> 🌐 www.bjgalbi.com
> ⑤⑤

Yangmiok 양미옥

The Euljiro area is full of venerable eateries, all boasting decades of know-how. Yangmiok is one such place, serving some of the city's best *gopchang-gui*, or grilled beef intestines, for 28 years at its Euljiro branch. The family-run operation is now into its second generation with the son heading a spanking new restaurant in Namdaemun that can handle up to 250 diners and special functions with its private dining rooms.

Yangmiok's *gopchang* is served Gyeongsang-do-style with its slightly sweet and spicy *gochujang* sauce. Beef intestines may not be for everyone so there's a *galbi*, or beef short ribs,

option. However, it would be a shame to miss out on Yangmiok's signature *yang-gopchang*, or beef blanket tripe. Unlike *gopchang*, it has little fat and boasts a chewy and crispy texture, bursting with umami flavors. What makes it so special is the quality of the tripe and the expert servers who grill it perfectly at the table, each and every time. Don't forget to finish your barbecue with either a *gopchang-jeongol* hot pot or a *doenjang-jjigae* stew.

> 📍 9-1, Namdaemun-ro 5-gil, Jung-gu
> 📞 02-3789-9288
> ⑤⑤

There are two types of *naengmyeon*, or cold noodle. One is *mul-naengmyeon* made with savory cold broth, the other is *bibim-naengmyeon* in a spicy *gochujang* sauce. *Naengmyeon* can also be categorized by region. Pyongyang *naengmyeon* has noodles made from buckwheat flour, resulting in a softer texture. Hamheung *naengmyeon* has noodles made from buckwheat flour mixed with potato starch, producing a much chewier experience. Though both the Pyongyang and Hamheung varieties include *mul* and *bibim* versions, the Pyongyang variety is more commonly enjoyed as *mul-naengmyeon* with a mild broth.

Woo Lae Oak 우래옥

Euljiro's (and perhaps the country's) top choices for *naengmyeon* are Eulji Myeonok and Woo Lae Oak. Woo Lae Oak is considered the oldest *naengmyeon* establishment in Korea, and, unlike other shops, its rich broth is made solely from beef. Folks love its rich, deep broth and the flavorful buckwheat noodles that make up their famous *mul-naengmyeon*. Their *bibim-naengmyeon* is known for a fairly large amount of kimchi added to the mix. Unlike other *naengmyeon* shops, this is an upscale *hansik* restaurant that is also renowned for its bulgogi, *galbi*, and beef tartare, or *yukhoe*.

> 📍 62-29, Changgyeonggung-ro, Jung-gu
> 📞 02-2265-0151
> ⑤~⑤⑤

Neung Ra Do 능라도

Compared with other popular Pyongyang *naengmyeon* joints, Neung Ra Do is a new name. The owner, Kim Young-chul, followed the wishes of his North Korea-born father who was a huge *naengmyeon* fan and opened his first branch in Pangyo in 2010. It may be less than a decade old, but it's a heavy hitter with branches all over the city. The Gangnam branch has received a Bib Gourmand in the Michelin guide. The *naengmyeon* broth at Neung Ra Do uses *hanu* beef cuts, including shanks, brisket and flank. Some pork is also added to the broth, as well as kombu dashi and shitake mushrooms for flavor. Neung Ra Do is also famous for its *eobokjaengban*, a hot pot featuring a glorious mountain of crown daisies and perilla leaves. After the first boil, however, you'll find beef slices hiding below. Some like to eat the beef slices wrapped with the greens, while others like to dip the meat and vegetables in the seasoning sauce. Add the *nokdu-jeon*, or mung bean pancakes, along with *mandu*, dumplings, into the hotpot.

📍 7, Eonju-ro 107-gil, Gangnam-gu
📞 02-569-8939
🌐 neungrado.modoo.at
⑤~⑤⑤

The Michelin Guide for Seoul is just into its third year but many Korean restaurants are getting some global attention. Here's a tip about making the Michelin rounds: try the lunch course. It's usually about half the price of dinner.

Zero Complex 제로 콤플렉스

Chef Lee Choong-hu was the youngest chef to be awarded a star in the Michelin Guide Seoul 2017. He was still in his twenties when he opened Zero Complex in 2014. It's difficult to box Chef Lee's food into a particular category. There are French influences from his days at Le Cordon Bleu and stints at renowned French restaurants, but his main sources of inspiration are his everyday experiences realized through weekly trips to a farm in Yeoju where he sources local seasonal vegetables. While much of the food is based on French classics, Chef Lee mixes in Korean ingredients and flavors he grew up with. Sometimes it leads to unexpected results, such as his endive and caramel mousse dish.

Always the risk-taker, Chef Lee moved after four years in Seocho-gu's Seorae Maeul to a new multi-concept space, Piknic, in Jung-gu. Zero Complex is found on the third floor, and there's a first floor café run by the popular Hell Cafe. Zero Complex plans to collaborate with Hell Cafe on the café menu, which includes light meals and tapas.

📍 3F, 30, Toegye-ro 6ga-gil, Jung-gu
📞 02-532-0876
ⓢⓢⓢ

Jungsik 정식당

Chef Yim Jungsik won the adoration of Korean foodies when he introduced his "Korean nouvelle" menu at Jungsik, opened in 2009. The dishes used local, seasonal ingredients with French cooking techniques and plating. Yim's Jungsik is often named as the first example of molecular gastronomy applied to *hansik* dishes. Not content to stay in the Korean dining scene, Yim opened a New York branch in 2011. All doubts were silenced in 2013 when Jungsik in New York earned its first Michelin star and was then recognized with two the following year. Jungsik in Seoul also won its two stars in 2017. Jungsik's menu is famous for its whimsical reinterpretations of common Korean dishes like *gimbap* and bibimbap. Chef Yim likes to cite his Delicious Gujeolpan as an example that going against tradition has its rewards. Jungsik's *gujeolpan*—a colorful platter of eight fillings wrapped in buckwheat crepes—uses *gimbugak*, or fried seasoned laver, and a variety of seasonal ingredients to create a more complex and delicious flavor profile than the traditional version.

Tip: There's the stylish Jungsik Bar on the first floor that often serves popular dishes from the upstairs dining menu.

📍 11, Seolleung-ro 158-gil, Gangnam-gu
📞 02-517-4654
🌐 www.jungsik.kr
💲💲💲

Joo Ok 주옥

Joo ok means "gem" or "jewel" in Korean and is often used to describe something precious. Chef Shin Chang-ho wanted his *hansik* bistro to pay careful attention to the ingredients and prepare food he would be proud to serve his own mother. He also wanted to reinterpret Korean food, not beholden to tradition, expressing his years of experience in French cuisine and work in restaurants abroad.

Chef Shin's attention to detail is found in the signature vinegar sampler served as the first course to awaken the diner's appetite and senses. Chef Shin makes them himself, and he's become

a bit of a vinegar fanatic over the years, concocting about 20 different versions. Another "*joo ok*" the dish named Perilla Oil which contains valuable ingredients like Russian caviar and abalone conch from Gangwon-do. But what makes it a stand-out gem is the perilla oil made from the seeds grown at his mother-in-law's farm. It's a small mouthful but an intensely rewarding one.

📍 52-7, Seolleung-ro 148-gil, Gangnam-gu
📞 02-518-9393
🌐 thejoook.modoo.at
⑤⑤⑤

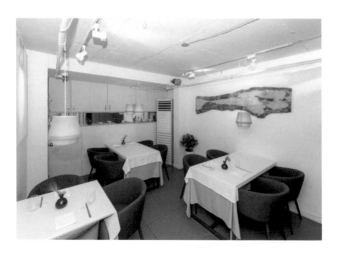

108

Bansang is the structure of a traditional Korean meal. *Bap*, or rice, is the main actor and *banchan* side dishes are the supporting players. There are rules on the placement of the dishes and even what each serving dish or utensil should be made of. Today's *bansang* meals don't obey these complicated rules to the letter, but many try follow the basic structure of providing a variety of flavors, textures and seasonal ingredients.

Moomyung Sikdang 무명식당

Moomyung means "no-name" in Korean. The idea behind the restaurant is that the menu shouldn't be colored by a certain regional cuisine or theme. Each *bansang* may feature *banchan* sides and soup from different parts of Korea. The focus is on healthy and well-balanced meals that use local and seasonal ingredients. While the original Seongbuk-dong branch opened in 2013, the franchise has quickly grown to various locations in and around Seoul.

Moomyung places special importance on *bap*. You won't find the usual sticky bland white rice packed into stainless steel bowls here. Eleven different grains go into Moomyung's signature mixed grains rice, and the Moomyung Bapsang set menu serves a combination of soup, meat dishes, kimchi, *jeotgal* (salted seafood), pickled vegetables and dried seaweed. There's also the Byeolmi Bapsang that includes regional specialties. Both set meals change daily.

> 📍 50, Seongbuk-ro, Seongbuk-gu
> 📞 T. 02-743-1733
> 💲

Yang Chul Cooking 양출쿠킹

Yang Chul Cooking is representative of the popular *jipbap* or homestyle diners sprouting all over the city. The original Apgujeong-dong branch is cozy and small with brick and wood interior accents, and there's a second branch nearby. The restaurant is named after the owner-chef who worked as an actress before moving to Japan to spend five years at culinary school. This education brings a Japanese influence to the menu, which offers a range of both *hansik* and Japanese dishes.

Yang Chul offers various *bansang* set meals that range from KRW 10,000 to 15,000. Each set meal comes with rice, soup and various *banchan* that change daily. *Deopbap* meals, rice with toppings like pickled pollack roe and wasabi, are also quite popular. In the evening, the menu focuses on *anju* dishes that pair well with Korean wine and liquor. Check their social media for special wine and liquor pairing events.

> 📍 15, Nonhyeon-ro 157-gil, Gangnam-gu
> 📞 02-547-4420
> 🌐 facebook.com/yangchulcooking
> ⓢ

Balwoo Gongyang 발우공양

Korea's temple cuisine has become a global leader in the world's slow food movement. Eric Ripert, star chef of New York's Le Bernardin, is a Buddhist and also a vocal fan of Korean temple cuisine, which he has described as the "parent of the slow food movement in the Western World."

Balwoo Gongyang opened in 2009 to introduce Koreans to its vegan cuisine that eschews pungent spices and flavors like garlic and chives. However, fermented foodstuffs and seasonings like *ganjang*, *doenjang* and *gochujang* add layers of flavors unmatched in other restaurants. The tasting courses are seasonal and diners can choose from a range of prices as cheap as KRW 30,000 for lunch. Alcohol is not served, but there's a choice of great teas and beverages, and corkage is available at dinner service.

> ⓞ 5F, Temple Stay Information Integration Center, 56, Ujeongguk-ro, Jongno-gu
> ☏ 02-733-2081
> ⊕ balwoo.or.kr
> ⑤⑤⑤

© Baroo Gongyang

Chinese diners may not recognize some of the Chinese dishes enjoyed here in Korea. Americans have their chop suey and General Tso's chicken, and Koreans have their *jjajangmyeon*, *tangsuyuk* and *mandu* (usually served on the house as "service").

Jin Jin 진진

Chef Wang Yuk-sung is one of the greats in Chinese cuisine, and for over 40 years, he has worked in some of the best restaurants in the city. He wanted Jin Jin to introduce traditional Chinese food at a more accessible location and at affordable prices. His efforts were rewarded with a Michelin star in 2018, and the original branch in Seogyo-dong has expanded to two more in the city. Reservations are highly recommended at any of their locations.

Jin Jin's signature dish, *menbosha*, may be a little unfamiliar, but it's basically minced shrimp stuffed between slices of sandwich bread, then deep-fried. It doesn't have the complexity of grand Chinese dishes, but with its crispy texture and savory shrimp stuffing, it's simply finger-licking good. And it's perfect with a bottle (or two) of Tsingtao. Another popular dish is the stir-fried snow crab meat. This savory dish, with a consistency somewhere between a soup and a sauce, is full of crab meat and addictively delicious. Don't forget to round out your meal with Jin Jin's popular *mul-mandu* (boiled dumplings). The dumplings here use thick wrappers and have a solid filling.

📍 123, Jandari-ro, Mapo-gu
📞 070-5035-8878
🌐 jinjinseoul.modoo.at
ⓢⓢ

Gwangjang Market 광장시장

It seems that nearly every tourist makes it to Gwangjang Market's main hall filled with hawkers selling piles of giant mung bean pancakes (*bindaetteok*), pork hocks, and, of course, *san nakji*—the small octopus, still very much alive, that provides the classic K-food challenge. Be ready to Instagram and YouTube your first wriggling octopus experience!

But there's more to the market than the giant main hall. It's still a working market, and if you explore other smaller halls and alleyways, you'll find that it's full of great cheap eats and drinking holes frequented by the market vendors and customers. The Michelin Guide agreed and awarded a Bib Gourmand to **Buchon Yukhoe** in the famous raw beef alley. It serves slices of raw beef seasoned with sesame oil over thin slices of pears, topped with a raw egg. Mix it all together for an umami flavor blast and order some *makgeolli* to wash it all down. Venture out into the less explored alleyways and expect the unexpected from the addictive *mayak* "drug" *gimbap* to *seonji-haejangguk*, a thick, spicy soup made from ox bone, coagulated blood, soybean paste and other healthy ingredients, often eaten after a night on the town to prevent a hangover.

> 88, Changgyeonggung-ro, Jongno-gu
> 02-2267-0291
> www.kwangjangmarket.co.kr
> ⓢ

Sejong Village Food Culture Street & Tongin Market 세종마을 음식문화거리와 통인시장

Seochon used to be a sleepy neighborhood where you could escape the downtown throng, but no longer. Recently, the government designated its Chebu-dong area as Sejong Village Food Culture Street. This long, winding road is filled with a diverse array of restaurants, bars and cafés, frequented by Gwanghwamun office workers, local hipsters, foreign tourists and even Gangnam day trippers. People watching here is almost as much fun as eating. Feeling some barbecue? There's **Oneungjeong Jjokgalbi**, with its huge outdoor barbecue grill, where the pork ribs are pre-grilled and pull you in with their delicious smoky aroma. Planning a big night out? Try the aptly named **Anju Maeul**, famous for its delectable food that's almost too good for soju. Chasing a hangover? Head to the 24 hour stand-by, **Chebu-dong Janchijip**, famous for its noodles with ground perilla seeds.

Also check out **Tongin Market**, famous for its *dosirak* system where you can fill a lunchbox with items from food stalls all over the market for a mere KRW 5,000.

📍 18, Jahamun-ro 15-gil, Jongno-gu
📞 02-722-0911
🌐 tonginmarket.modoo.at
$~$$

The Old Noryangjin

Noryangjin Market 노량진 수산시장

The Noryangjin Fisheries Wholesale Market opened its new market building in 2016, but due to some controversy over the new facilities among the organizers and vendors, the old market is still open for business next door, and visitors hoping to score the freshest fish and seafood in town have their choice between the two. The new market is not yet at full capacity, but there are many seafood stalls on the first floor and restaurants on the second.

It can be quite daunting to bargain with experienced vendors, surrounded by the sensory onslaught of the Noryangjin Market, old or new. It pays to do some research on the preferred fish: the average weights for young or mature fish, the average going rate and if they are in season. Luckily, there is an app (tpirates.com) that lists daily market rates and also offers delivery services.

Tip: *Yangnyeom sikdang* restaurants in the market will prepare your freshly purchased seafood and provide a table setting to enjoy the meal for a fee. A typical table setting for *hoe*, or sashimi, or barbecue might run about KRW 10,000 per person. A pot of *maeuntang*, a spicy stew made from the bones and leftover meat from your fish, to round out the meal may be an extra KRW 10,000 to 20,000, depending on the number of diners.

📍 674, Nodeul-ro, Dongjak-gu
📞 02-2254-8000
🌐 www.susansijang.co.kr
$ $

Gwanghwamun Gukbap 광화문국밥

Chef Park Chan-il reinterprets the ultimate Korean soul food, *gukbap*, for a new generation. Chef Park has taken a few U-turns in his career, from journalist to Italian chef and now food writer and Korean comfort food restaurateur. Gwanghwamun Gukbap wants to set the Seoul standard of Korea's ultimate fast food: soup and rice. It's a working class dish, but Chef Park has set the bar high. Instead of masking lower quality ingredients with spicy seasoning, Chef Park has chosen rich Berkshire K-pork for the soup and *suyuk*, or steamed meat platter, and serves Koshihikari rice from the Icheon region. Similar care has been put into the restaurant interior. There's a stylish-retro feel to the green and beige walls and stainless steel tabletops. A long communal table welcomes single diners looking for a quick but comforting meal.

Groups are welcome too, and the menu features a short list of *anju* dishes like *soondae* (blood sausage), *suyuk*, and pollack roe and cucumber *muchim* that would go well with soju and *makgeolli*.

📍 53, Sejong-daero 21-gil, Jung-gu
📞 02-738-5688
ⓢ

Jaha Sonmandu 자하손만두

Famous for its lovely views and quality food, Jaha Sonmandu is the place for dumplings. Hikers and bikers often finish their morning treks up and down Inwangsan Mountain over a hearty bowl of *mandutguk* here. The main dining room has views of Inwangsan that provide a rustic backdrop to the hearty dumplings made on site with minced beef and pork, bean sprouts and tofu. It's a simple bowl of soup and dumplings, but there's attention to detail. The beef broth for the *mandutguk* is not too rich and is seasoned with homemade *ganjang*, or soy sauce.

On any given weekend, diners wait in the courtyard of the restaurant surrounded by large earthenware bowls filled with *ganjang* and other fermented seasonings. They come for another crowd favorite—the *tteok-mandutguk*, warm soup filled with round pieces of rice cake along with smaller dumplings in an array of pink, yellow and green. It's simple but lovely, and filling to boot.

> 📍 12, Baekseokdong-gil, Jongno-gu
> 📞 02-379-2648
> $

Joseon Gimbap 조선김밥

Mom knows best, especially when it comes to *gimbap*. It's a perfectly packable food, made with a mother's loving care. But these days, even moms need a break, and families go to premium *gimbap* shops for the latest trends in *gimbap*. Ingredients here aren't limited to the usual suspects of egg, carrots and *danmuji* (pickled radish). Now it's all about *tonkatsu*, wasabi shrimp, cream cheese and *hanu* bulgogi.

Joseon Gimbap, one such premium *gimbap* joint, serves different seasonal *gimbap* rolls using high quality ingredients. Seasoned vegetables, or *namul*, are big players in their flavor profiles. *Eomuk* fishcakes are often served boiled in seafood stock or mixed in with *tteokbokki*, but at Joseon Gimbap, they find a new home in the popular Odeng Gimbap. There's wasabi tucked between the *eomuk* layers, creating a unique flavor mix that many folks have grown to love. Tip: If you order for take-out, you'll save 500 won.

📍 78, Yulgok-ro 1-gil, Jongno-gu
📞 02-723-7496
💲

Sona 소나

Pastry Chef Seong Hyunah's Sona has a simple motto: "Make desserts better." It's superbly realized in the dessert tasting menus that display Chef Seong's creativity and flair. The café aims to bring the quality of desserts served in fine dining establishments to a wider public in a more casual setting.

One such example is her signature Champagne Snow Ball dessert, which is almost too lovely to eat. A light pink sugar ball encases rose sparkling foam, topped with flower petals and olive oil powder. The delicate snowball rests on creamy strawberry panna cotta, fresh strawberry slices, cheesecake snow and milk snow. This extraordinary dessert resembles the holiday snow globes children grew up with. Now, grown-ups can indulge in their childhood memories through this delectable dessert. Chef Seong also developed a *haejang* drink to help customers recover from hangovers. Her Gingerfloat uses homemade ginger ale, honey, egg yolk and bananas to relieve fatigue.

📍 40, Gangnam-daero 162-gil, Gangnam-gu
📞 02-515-3246
🌐 facebook.com/sonadessert
ⓢ

Korean Eats with
Chef Yim Jung-sik

© Jungsik

Often credited with pioneering New Korean cuisine abroad and bringing fine dining to Korea, Chef Yim Jung-sik's reputation precedes him. Critically acclaimed by *The New York Times*, Zagat and Asia's 50 Best Restaurants, his Jungsik restaurants in New York and Seoul have both been awarded two Michelin stars. More recently, Chef Yim has been busy perfecting simpler Korean dishes at Pyeonghwaok, his latest venture specializing in beef bone soup, or *gomtang*, and cold buckwheat noodles, or *naengmyeon*.

Have you always liked eating out?

I liked eating out when I was younger. I still like it. I like all the things that average Koreans like—meat, raw fish and places that are good for drinking. Before I started running a restaurant, I'd look up blogs and visit the best restaurants. I went to the legends on Jongno and Dongdaemun's Grilled Fish Street, Jinokhwa Halmae Wonjo Dakhanmari and all the places on the *dakhanmari* (whole chicken stew) alley.

Is it true that you visited all the best *gomtang* restaurants before opening Pyeonghwaok?

I thought a lot about what dishes are representative of Korea. In the morning, Koreans love to have rice in their soup. I saw how integrated rice-in-soup is to the Korean lifestyle, so I wanted to work with *gomtang*. *Naengmyeon* came along because Koreans are the only ones to eat noodles in a cold broth. That concept doesn't really exist in other cultures. Of course, there's soba but you don't really eat that immersed in the broth.

Do you have any favorites among them?

I like Jinmi Pyeongyang Nangmyeon. I like Woo Lae Oak. I really like Neung Ra Do. All the *naengmyeon* fanatics are crazy about it. It's one of those restaurants that do such a good job and have a really good system in place. They started in Bundang and now they have branches in Mapo, Ilsan and more. All of their branches are consistent in their quality.

What kind of restaurants would you recommend to people visiting Korea?

I think that tourists should try their best to have real Korean food. There are so many choices. When I have friends visit, I take them to *samgyeopsal* restaurants. I think a lot of people really like Korean barbecue. I also like to introduce hangover soup. In terms of restaurants, Bongpiyang has all the representative foods. They sell meat and they have all the soupy dishes like *kimchi-jiggae*, *doenjang-jiggae*, *gomtang* and *naengmyeon*. Their pork ribs are really delicious.

How about for vegetarians?

It's so hard for vegetarians to eat out. When it comes to vegetarian food, I recommend this place in Gangwon-do called Buil Sikdang. They sell *sanchae baekban* (rice with seasoned wild vegetables) and they cover the table with twenty kinds of side dishes. It's completely vegetarian! Vegan even!

What do you think about *banchan* (side dishes) being free?

I think people need to pay for *banchan* in the future. Most people leave so much food behind not realizing how much effort and cost goes into each side dish. When it's free and people get refills, so much goes to waste. From the restaurant's perspective, it's like giving away twenty tapas.

Do you think that people evaluate Pyeonghwaok differently from Jungsik because Pyeonghwaok's dishes are so much more familiar to the average Korean?

Because Jungsik's food has so much character, it's hard to compare it to anything else. But the food we make at Pyeonghwaok is always being compared. There are people who really like us and people who really dislike us. Even my mom gives me very objective reviews. The noodles are like this, the portions are too big, the kimchi is too ripe. I'm still in the process of listening to all our customers. I see what people are saying on Instagram. Of course,

I don't take all the suggestions people give but I consider them. I have a philosophy to my food and I don't think everyone has the same philosophy.

Do you ever just eat *ramyeon* or *gimbap*?

After work, I often grab a triangle *gimbap* from the convenience store. This happens twice a week. Tuna-mayo sells the best and I think there's a reason for that. Tuna-mayo-bacon, a new flavor, is my favorite. Since I cook for work, there are some days when I don't feel like doing anything. If I get hungry, I cook two *ramyeon* and pour Tabasco all over it. Then it's spicy and sour. Tabasco *ramyeon* is even on the Jungsik bar menu.

Written by **Hahna Yoon**

The Philosopher Chef:
Jeong Kwan

At first glance, Jeong Kwan is a diminutive middle-aged woman with an unassuming demeanor, and on the day of our interview, a week-long flu and a punishing schedule of interviews and cooking classes had left her exhausted with a sore phlegmy throat. But when she launches into the meaning of food in her life and her practice of Buddhism, she speaks with a confident forcefulness that reminds you of her reputation as the world's greatest chef—the philosopher chef.

"I choose to work with the public and communicate with them," explains Jeong Kwan. "Whatever title they give me is not important. It's my passion to share through food so I don't feel tired. I always want to be open and share all of myself with the world."

And the world is keen to know her. Jeong Kwan has been the face of Korea's temple food, featured on documentaries with Michelin-star chef Eric Ripert, celebrated in NYT features, and lauded in the Netflix documentary *Chef's Table*, which coined the "philosopher chef" nickname.

"It's part of our Buddhist mission to communicate with the world about food and Buddhism," she explains. Teaching is also part of her mission. "Every Sunday, 15 to 20 foreigners come to learn about temple food from me, but I don't speak English," she smiles. At the Templestay program at Cheonjinam Hermitage, a quiet Buddhist hermitage in the serene mountainous monastery of Baekyangsa Temple, they learn together about food, culture, nature and Buddhism. "Everyone is different with their culture, lifestyle and language," she says. "But the energy we share is one. The world is one."

Food as meditation

For Jeong Kwan, food is a tool of meditation and self-realization. She begins with gratitude and love for the heaven and sky, and the farmer for their labor to provide the ingredients. "Food is wisdom," she says. "You have to understand the ingredients, and from that comes wisdom." She takes *chwinamul*, or seasoned aster, as an example. "Its character changes dramatically from March to April to May. To season and cook it, you have to understand it." She continues that applying devotion to your understanding of ingredients is part of your relationship to nature, and cooking becomes a "creative act." Making food is then an act of creativity and self-realization—to find your true self.

Fermented food is also described as a philosophical, metaphysical journey. "Salt and water are added to the ingredients and then it's stored and fermented," she says. "With time and energy, it becomes fermented food like *doenjang* and *ganjang*." She continues, "They change through time itself, with the energy of time. It's neither human nor nature."

Listening to Jeong Kwan, it's easy to understand why chefs like Eric Ripert are drawn to her. She gives meaning to the everyday mundane work of cooking and makes it rise above its ephemeral qualities. A lifetime of devotion to food has given her insight that she now wants to share with the world. She teaches at Cheonjinam Hermitage and also at the Korean Temple Food Center in Seoul. Associated with over six different organizations, she gives interviews and talks in Korea and abroad.

Food is about sharing

Jeong Kwan's long list of duties makes her busier than most celebrities and while she wouldn't admit she's worn out, she's decided to take some time for herself. "I want to take three months in winter, to travel the world and see if it's just me who feels this way about food," she says. Her first such tour was last winter. She traveled to Europe and North America, and it was an eye-opening experience. "In Europe, so many people had their own gardens and farms. They're very

© Cultural Corps of Korean Buddhism

interested in food and temple cuisine. They have passion for the essence of food. Not just about recipes and flavors, but about the essence of the ingredients."

Jeong Kwan's face lights up when she describes her visit to a family in San Diego last year. "The family visited me in Cheonjinam after they saw the Netflix documentary. So I visited them at their home in California without any notice. When I arrived, their seven-year-old daughter took me barefoot through their garden. She described each and every plant, 58 of them, in her garden. She had helped her parents and brother plant and harvest each vegetable. The little girl then helped her family cook what she harvested. She was so happy to do it." Jeong Kwan thought about her garden and she felt ashamed. "Here's this seven-year-old without any pretense, paying so much attention to her food and acting on it."

It made Jeong Kwan realize that she wasn't alone in her passion for food and that she would make her journey abroad to discover people like her. "Food is about sharing. I want to share how to make food." She laughs when asked if she would write a cooking book. "Look around, the bookshelves are filled with recipe books." Then she grows thoughtful. "Maybe a book about food ingredients." Her eyes twinkle and she grows excited. "Plants change in flavor in just a few weeks. And there are so many of them. There could be something in that."

Written by **Cynthia Yoo**

Cafés & Teashops

Spending a leisurely hour or two at a café is one of the most local things you can do in Seoul. Locals can spend entire days at cafés talking to friends or doing work. The coffee boom of the past decade means that you can easily find a café on every street corner, and likely a decent one at that. Some spaces prioritize coffee over design, others emphasize ambiance, and a few bring together the best of both worlds to create a small slice of heaven. The Itaewon, Mangwon-dong and Seochon neighborhoods lend themselves to café hopping. Tea lovers, on the other hand, may find the best leaves in downtown Seoul's more historical neighborhoods. Many teahouses themselves have a great story to tell.

Choose a local shop over a big corporate chain and you won't be disappointed.

Anthracite

The café to impress the hardest to please, Anthracite is one of the most exciting names in Korea's coffee scene. Their reputation of marrying good beans and intense ambiance began in Hapjeong-dong in 2010 when owner Kim Pyoung-rae, recently returned from his studies in the US and, inspired by its jazz cafés, set out to create a space in which people could drink good coffee and enjoy music. In his quest, Kim found an abandoned shoe warehouse that he renovated himself and filled with artistically inclined baristas. Since then, three more Anthracites have opened in Seoul, each carrying a strong presence. Single-origin coffees are poured over on conveyor belts that double as counter space at the Hapjeong-dong branch. A large indoor garden graces the second floor of the Hannam-dong branch. The recent addition, the Seogyo-dong branch, is an introvert's dream. The location's high ceilings and natural wood come with unlimited coffee and strict rules to speak softly.

Hapjeong	Seogyo
📍 10, Tojeong-ro 5-gil, Mapo-gu	📍 11, World Cup-ro 12-gil, Mapo-gu
📞 02-322-7009	📞 02-322-7009
Hannam	**Yeonhui**
📍 240, Itaewon-ro, Yongsan-gu	📍 135, Yeonhui-ro, Seodaemun-gu
📞 02-797-7009	📞 02-332-7991
🌐 anthracitecoffee.com	

MANUFACT COFFEE COLD BREW SYSTEM

Manufact

With three different locations across Seoul, Manufact is the coffee for those who like their drinks cold and reasonably priced. At the original Yeonhui-dong location, the aroma hits you as soon as you get past the crowd. It's the popularity of this small roaster that helped grow Manufact into what it is today. Flat whites are properly done, hand-drip coffees are consistently perfect and the KRW 3,000 iced Paul Gauguin blend Americano is just as balanced and chocolaty as it promises to be. Although the Yeonhui-dong location has the best coffee, the Dosan Park and Bangbae-dong locations earn praise for their design as well as for their brews. Designed by fashion designers Kang Jin-young and Yoon Han-hee, Manufact's Dosan Park location is perched on the fourth floor veranda of the Queenmama Market concept store. With plenty of green space and an impressive cold brew system, it's our pick of the three if you're looking to sit awhile.

Yeonhui	Dosan Park	Bangbae
📍 29, Yeonhui-ro 11-gil, Seodaemun-gu	**(Queenmama Market)**	📍 15, Seocho-daero 27-gil. Seocho-gu
📞 02-6406-8777	📍 4F, 50, Apgujeong-ro 46-gil, Gangnam-gu	📞 02-535-0804
	📞 02-3442-0914	

🌐 manufactcoffee.com

Namusairo 나무사이로

Often appearing on lists of Seoul's best coffee, this café in a renovated *hanok* touts the motto "Great coffee starts with great ingredients. Quality is not an option. It is a must." The café's name means "through the trees" and was inspired by Kim Hwal-sung's poem "Path." Though originally opened in Sillim-dong in 2002, Namusairo has been at its current Sajik-dong location since 2013—close enough to Gwanghwamun to make it convenient but far enough to ensure that tourists don't overrun it. The quiet establishment boasts traditional ambiance in combination with rare, imported beans. Namely, the café serves the elusive

Panama Geisha, known as the world's most expensive coffee, for a whopping KRW 30,000 a cup. The menu also includes your standard Americanos, lattes and hand-drips for far more reasonable prices, curated by the café's acclaimed lead roaster, Bae Jun-sun. Take the drink of your choice into the *hanok's* airy courtyard and it's nearly impossible to have a sub-par experience.

📍 21, Sajik-ro 8-gil, Jongno-gu
📞 070-7590-0885
🌐 namusairo.com

Coffee Libre

Famous for revolutionizing Korea's coffee scene, Coffee Libre is credited with many firsts when it comes to the coffee scene in Seoul. Not only was it the first café in the country to serve specialty coffee, it may have also been the first place to serve a decent cup of joe, period. The brand's CEO, Seu Pil-hoon, was the first Korean to earn a Q-grader license in 2008. He opened Coffee Libre a year later as a hole-in-the-wall space in Yeonnam-dong, before the neighborhood was an "it" destination. Although Seu travels around the world, often purchasing beans directly from farmers, the original location remains unpretentious. The venue's cozy and aromatic atmosphere and its simple menu of espresso, Americano, latte, single-origin brews and hot chocolate remain unchanged, despite the appearance of scores of nearby competitors. Coffee Libre locations can now be found in Myeong-dong, Yeongdeungpo Times Square, Gangnam and Guatemala, and a portion of the café's profits goes to developing education in Honduras and India.

> 198, Seongmisan-ro, Mapo-gu
> 02-334-0615
> coffeelibre.kr

Fritz Coffee Company

If you can't tell by all the merchandise at the entrance of the Doha-dong branch, Fritz Coffee Company is more than just a coffee house—it's a brand, and a popular one at that. Though owner Kim Byung-ki says "Fritz" carries no particular meaning, that hasn't stopped scores of customers from purchasing T-shirts, cellphone cases and posters with Fritz' logo or mascot: a very cute blue seal. A collaborative effort between Kim, pastry chef Heo Min-su and a few award-winning baristas, the original Dohwa-dong location—a two-story brick house with a front yard—offers a wide selection of French breads and coffees. Purchasing beans directly from a handful of coffee farms in Central America and India, Fritz takes particular pride in its specialty coffee, though many argue the delicious pain au chocolat is its real selling point. Fritz's Yangjae-dong location is refreshingly residential, but its Arario Museum location in Wonseo-dong is a great place to pop in for some coffee and snacks on a touristy day.

Dohwa	Wonseo	Yangjae
📍 17, Saechang-ro 2-gil, Mapo-gu	📍 83, Yulgok-ro, Jongno-gu	📍 24-11, Gangnam-daero 37-gil, Seocho-gu
📞 02-3275-2045	📞 02-747-8101	📞 02-521-4148

🌐 fritz.co.kr

Ikovox Coffee

Named after the legendary cinema speakers from Zeiss Ikon, Ikovox Coffee earned its reputation as Garosu-gil's first good coffee shop when it was featured in a 2011 issue of *Monocle*. Since then, Ikovox has continued to woo customers into their Garosu-gil location and even opened four more locations in Seoul and Gyeonggi-do. Conjuring up images of sharpened No. 2 pencils and empty composition notebooks, Ikovox leans into its simple schoolhouse aesthetic with stiff chairs and hardwood desks. Freshly roasted beans are delivered to each location daily, so the coffee itself is ideal for coffee lovers who know how they like their brew. Customers can choose from an extensive menu of single origin coffee, non-coffee beverages and teas and decide on the roast of their beans. Overwhelmed by all the decisions? Feel free to ask one of the knowledgeable baristas—just let them know which tastes you prefer. Make sure to also check out the cakes on display, which come from famous dessert shop Glamorous Penguin.

> 37, Apgujeong-ro 10-gil, Gangnam-gu
> 02-545-2010

Alex the Coffee

A collaborative effort between architects Axis Design, design studio S/O Project and food consultants La Cuisine, Alex the Coffee earns accolades for its excellent coffee and its delightfully simple space. Under the motto "Specialty Coffee, Sourcing to Roasting," Alex the Coffee has four locations in Korea: one in Seoul's Seongbuk-dong neighborhood and three more in the nearby cities of Yongin, Ilsan and Icheon. Although the Yongin location helped to distinguish the brand back in 2013 with the Red Dot Award, the Seongbuk-dong location mirrors the minimalist aesthetic and serves equally delicious coffee. You can taste Alex' vibrant flavor in a simple Americano, but signature drinks such as the Alexano, the Fat Americano and the White Blanc demonstrate their ability to innovate as well. Make the best of the experience and take a seat upstairs in the café's greenhouse, where the sun shines shamelessly.

9, Seongbuk-ro 28-gil, Seongbuk-gu
070-7520-7714
alexthecoffee.com

Sikmul

Many credit this Ikseon-dong café-and-bar with putting the trendy neighborhood on the map. In renovating several old *hanok*, photographer and art director Louis Park fell in love with the narrow *hanok*-lined streets and did his best to create a space that, though modern, still made you feel nostalgic for the Korea of old. The space is divided up into several separate worlds: At one end of the café, you can sit cross-legged at antique Korean-style tables, while another corner looks like a poster straight out of 1970s America. Details like disco lights, vintage china and *hanok* tiles, the last one cemented directly into the walls, truly make Sikmul the café for lovers of atmosphere. The menu includes a list of decently priced wines, munchies, coffee and a few cocktails. The Boy and Girl, their signature coffee cocktails, are creamy concoctions not to be missed.

📍 46-1, Donhwamun-ro 11da-gil, Jongno-gu
📞 02-742-7582
🌐 www.instagram.com/sikmul

or.er.

Even in sea of trendy cafés that is Seongsu-dong, or.er. really stands out, so much so that *Vogue Korea* recently called the café "the world's most beautiful store." Taking its name from the etymology of the suffixes "-or" and "-er," which mean "someone who does something," or.er. is the second concept space of Zagmachi, one of the first hip spaces to open in Seongsu-dong. Home to a gallery, garden, lounge and design store, or.er. has a classic beauty that sets it apart from other concept-heavy spaces. Guests are welcome to order from a menu that includes teas, coffees and handmade cakes and enjoy themselves amid 1970s wallpaper and dark wooden furniture. The summery garden space is perfect for intimate chats with friends while the sturdy, spacious seating available on the second floor makes it the perfect place for larger outings and group projects. Don't forget to peep into the shop on the third floor where household items such as unique vases, glassware and other decorative trinkets are on sale.

> 📍 18, Yeonmujang-gil, Seongdong-gu
> 📞 02-462-0018
> 🌐 www.instagram.com/or.er

Onion

You can't talk about Seongsu-dong without mentioning café Onion. Though the industrial chic of the renovated factory is common in this part of town, few pull off the aesthetic so well. Facing a car detailing shop, the two-story venue has a selection of baked goods and coffee, a range of seating options and a popular second-floor rooftop. Part of the café's charm comes from the history of the 1970s building, which was a metalworking shop, a supermarket and a restaurant. Unlike other venues where exposed concrete is but one part of the interior, the concrete here is omnipresent.

Even so, there are so many nooks and crannies carved out of the concrete that you constantly feel as if you're discovering new dimensions. The coffee is always fresh but the popular ciabatta bread may sell out by the afternoon depending on the crowds, which are constant.

> 8, Achasan-ro 9-gil, Seongdong-gu
> 02-1644-1941
> www.instagram.com/cafe.onion

Cha-teul 차마시는뜰

Bukchon Hanok Village's Cha-teul excels with its selection of teas and unparalleled views. Its name short for Cha Masineun Teul, or "garden for drinking tea," the café is a *hanok* perched on a hill overlooking Samcheong-dong. In the *hanok's* courtyard, there's a luscious garden that remains colorful throughout the year. Be adventurous and order something other than the green tea. Better yet, talk to your server about any discomfort you've had, such as stress or indigestion, and they'll recommend a tea to help. Floral teas, Chinese teas, coffee and a small selection of snacks are also on the menu—the deep-fried sweet rice balls and the red-bean milk *bingsu* are two of the tastiest.

⚬ 26, Bukchon-ro 11na-gil, Jongno-gu
☏ T. 02-722-7006

Tteuran Tea House 뜰안

Though this café's first claim to fame was its appearance in the 2009 Korean-Japanese film *Café Seoul*, Ikseon-dong's Tteuran Tea House has remained relevant with its consistently good tea and warm atmosphere. Owner Kim Ae-ran, who renovated the *hanok* with her family in 2008, is one the most visible names in the Korean tea café scene and has been one of the keenest promoters of the Ikseon-dong neighborhood over the years. Maps of Ikseon-dong and magazines featuring the neighborhood crowd the counter space that separates the table seating from the kitchen. The best seats are, by far, the floor seats with views of the café's courtyard garden. Imperfectly manicured with out-of-control vines, the homey green patch is one of the café's highlights. Tteuran's Mulberry Shaved Ice comes highly recommended in the summer; for those who like red bean, the red bean porridge is a winter delicacy.

> 17-35, Supyo-ro 28-gil, Jongno-gu
> 02-745-7420

Osulloc 오설록

Cosmetic giant Amorepacific has its own tea brand, Osulloc, supplied by the company's large tea plantations on the southern island of Jeju. Osulloc's several spaces in Seoul offer excellent teas and tea-based beverages in sophisticated surroundings that combine traditional grace with contemporary sensibility. They serve tasty desserts made using tea, too, such as roll cakes, ice cream and shaved ice. Try the scones served with green tea milk spread. Osulloc 1979, on the ground floor of Amorepacific's spectacular new headquarters in Yongsan, is not only a beautiful space in in its own right, but also serves as an excuse to visit the trendy Amorepacific Museum of Art, located in the same building.

> 📍 100, Hangang-daero, Yongsan-gu
> 📞 070-5172-1171
> 🌐 www.osulloc.com

Talking Joe with
Coffee Magazine's Hong Sung-dae

One of the best-known names in the Korean coffee scene, Hong Sung-dae runs the publishing company IBLINE, the publisher of the monthly print magazine *Coffee* and the Korean edition of New York coffee magazine *Drift*. Hong sat down with us to discuss the development of Korea's coffee scene and explain what Koreans look for in their brew.

How has coffee in Korea changed over time?

In 1988, when Korea hosted the Olympics, there was little diversity in the types of coffee you could get in Korea. It was a matter of which instant coffee you preferred and maybe what kind of cream you took. In 1999, when Starbucks opened their first location in Korea near Ewha Womans University, we were introduced to Italian-style espresso and take-out coffee. Having a cup to go was completely new; there was something fashionable about it. Then Shinsegae got involved and formed a joint venture with Starbucks. A single private venture alone wouldn't have been able to lead the industry.

When was your first good cup of coffee?

Around the year 2000, I had an industry friend whom I first met at the International Bakery Association event in Germany. He imported espresso machines. After we came back to Korea, he invited me over to try some coffee. I don't know how I could put that taste in words. Maybe profound and mysterious? I thought, "If this is what coffee could always be, it'd be worth exploring."

How would you describe Korea's café scene?

The competition is intense. Coffee makers specialize their menus and constantly work on taste. A visitor to Seoul can easily find a good cup of coffee. There are an estimated 9,000 cafés in Korea. Good cafés are popping up all over Daegu and Busan, too. Jeju has more cafés per person than anywhere else in Korea—there are almost 2,000 there. We're working on an issue about it. We're curious to know what Jeju's locals think about all the change.

How much coffee do you drink in a day? What's the most expensive coffee you've ever had?

About three cups of a day. I'm never tired of it. The most expensive coffee I've ever had was the Kopi Luwak. It owes its price to scarcity, not flavor. The coffee beans include coffee cherries that have been digested by the Asian palm civet. One cup is KRW 50,000 at the Shilla Hotel. Most experts, however, find it underwhelming. Nowadays, I really like Geisha coffee, even if I can't drink it every day. It's also expensive, though not nearly as so as the Luwak. A cup of Geisha coffee tastes great and its beans are gorgeous. They serve it at Namusairo, one of my favorite cafés. I'm quite close with the owner there, too.

You often go overseas. What kind of coffee or bean do you hope comes to Korea?

When I go to Milan, I avoid all the great places to drink coffee. Instead, I think about what the average cup of coffee is like. I believe that the average cup of coffee in Milan isn't as good as the average cup of coffee in Seoul. It's like kimchi. For Koreans, kimchi is an essential side dish. Of course, we rate kimchi and talk about which restaurant serves the best. Overall, though, we see it as simply a part of our daily lives. That's how I felt the Milanese viewed their coffee. Of course, Milan has really good cafés, too, particularly around the Duomo. I think the best coffee in Italy is at highway rest stops. Prepared by skilled baristas, it is consistently fresh and delicious.

Written by **Hahna Yoon**

Nightlife

Seoul is a famously 24-hour city with a broad range of nightlife activities. Whatever your flavor, the city will provide. The local drinking scene is as vast as the ocean is wide. Whether it's sipping single malts in rarefied surroundings or getting hammered on cheap soju to the break of dawn, you'll find endless options. The cocktail scene is exploding thanks to world-class bartenders, and even traditional Korean alcohol is experiencing a welcome revival.

Wanna party? Young Korean DJs spin everything from alternative hip-hop to ambient dubstep. At the bigger clubs, well-known international acts play before wild crowds. Though Hapjeong, Itaewon and Gangnam are the city's hottest spots at night, especially for clubbing, you can find plenty of great little bars throughout the city. Be prepared to make it a late night!

Cakeshop

Named after the famous Cake Shop in New York, this legendary hip-hop club could be credited with turning Itaewon into the new nightlife center of Seoul. Small and unknown when it first opened in 2012, the basement club really took off after Korean and foreign celebrities alike began getting tables here—rumor had it that it was one of G-Dragon's favorite spots. Although the exclusive, music-maniac feel of the club has disappeared some, crowds of young hip-hoppers fill up a good party here every weekend. Past international acts have included James Blake, Mannie Fresh and Jean Tonique, and anyone's whose anyone in the local hip-hop scene has spun here. For a more laid-back Cakeshop, check out the venue on a Thursday night or head to one of Cakeshop's affiliate locations—Contra, upstairs, and Pistil, down the street.

- 134, Itaewon-ro, Yongsan-gu
- T. 02-7444-1926
- Entry is KRW 20,000 with a free drink.
- www.cakeshopseoul.com

© Cakeshop

© Cakeshop

© Cakeshop

© Soap, Kai Paparazzi

Soap

Since opening in 2017, this underground hip-hop and electronic club has developed a reputation for throwing the hottest parties and the most talked-about events. The group that founded the club, Pute Deluxe, includes two big names in the Seoul nightlife scene, entertainer Julian Quintart and DJ Yann Cavaille. Specializing in pop-up events at rooftops around the city for a few years, once drawing 1,800 people to a party, Pute Deluxe continues to brand themselves with their music and products.

Shaped like a bar of soap, the club is lit up with blue lights and fully equipped with a VOID sound system. Past performers here have included LA-based producer Yung Bae, Korean-American rapper Dumbfoundead and DJ Shintaro, the 2013 Red Bull Thre3Style world champion. Be prepared to stand in line to get in if there's a big-name performer in town.

📍 14-9, Bogwang-ro 60-gil, Yongsan-gu

📞 070-4457-6860

💬 Entry is KRW 20,000 with a free drink.

🌐 soapseoul.com

Octagon

The quintessential Gangnam mega club, Octagon is decadent, posh and loud. Able to hold up to 3,000 people, the mostly electronic-music club is the go-to destination for large crowds and after-parties. Often in the top ten of DJ Mag's prestigious Top 100 Clubs list, the club is no stranger to names like Tiësto, Hardwell, Skrillex, Jamie Foxx and Steve Aoki. The Funktion-One sound system doesn't hurt, either.

Though the private rooms in the VIP area overlooking the main stage may be appealing, the real party is downstairs where disco lights and confetti dance with the merrymakers. The drinks on the menu are nothing to boast about, though. Clubbers on a budget head to the convenience store next door for pre-clubbing pregaming. Be sure to dress to impress—the club is notorious for turning people away at the door. No back on your shoes? No identification? Too "old"? Good luck!

⦿ 645, Nonhyeon-ro, Gangnam-gu
☏ 02-516-8847
◉ Entry is KRW 30,000 with two free drinks.
⊕ www.octagonseoul.com

© Octagon

© Vurt

Vurt

Located in the basement of a commercial building in Hapjeong-dong, this techno-music club has been likened to a concrete bunker. Unlike other venues that heavily promote foreign DJs, Vurt opened in 2014 with the mission to bring the "Ancient Future" of music to Seoul, focusing on up-and-coming local talent. Its roster of DJs includes key players in the Korean techno scene, artists such as Suna and Djilogue. In spite of the local line-up, the intense, industrial ambiance combines with the deep-techno sounds to give Vurt an unmistakable Berlin-esque feel.

With many music-lovers here to actually hear the riffs, there's less mingling and less activity on the dance floor than at other clubs. If techno's your scene, however, it's a great place to start getting involved and meet people with similar interests.

- 11, Dongmak-ro, Mapo-gu
- 02-3142-1356
- Entry is KRW 20,000 with a free drink.
- facebook.com/vurtkr

Brown Soul/Seoul

Although hip-hop has exploded in Seoul, the public's taste in music is a work in progress. That is to say, you'd still be hard-pressed to find a club in the Hongdae area without LMFAO's "Party Rock Anthem" on the playlist. Hapjeong's Brown Soul/Seoul, however, has earned the respect of music snobs. Although the club and lounge puts an emphasis on old-school hip-hop, they touch on everything from R&B, funk and dancehall to soul. DJs Jaysoul and Lockfly have particularly good taste in music. Though its small space—just a small bar and a dance floor with a disco ball at the center—fills up on Friday and Saturday nights, rumor has it that the best parties take place on Thursdays. With YG Entertainment not too far away, it's rife with opportunities to mingle with people in the business.

📍 B1, 21 Yanghwa-ro 6-gil, Mapo-gu

📞 02-3141-2330

💲 Entry is KRW 15,000 with a free drink on Fri and Sat. Free on Sun to Thu. Closed on Mon.

🌐 facebook.com/brownsoulseoul

Channel 1969

This bar, performance hall and music club describes itself as "an illustrious live bar" welcoming all kinds of people and all genres of music. One of Yeonnam-dong's few dancing spaces, Channel 1969 is warm and inviting. On weeknights, the plush seating lets groups catch up over drinks; on the weekend, the vibe very much depends on what's being hosted. Events range from indie-music concerts and electronic-DJ sets to metal and noise rock, with crowds an eclectic mix of people from different backgrounds. During the summer, clubbers gather outside the bar for convenience store beers and cigarettes. The environment's ripe for meeting new people and exchanging phone numbers, making Channel 1969 one of the most welcoming spots for newcomers and singles.

📍 35, Yeonhui-ro, Mapo-gu

📞 010-5581-1112

🕐 Entry depends on events.

🌐 facebook.com/channel.1969.seoul

Seendosi 신도시

When you visit Seendosi for the first time, it feels like you're walking onto the set of Blade Runner rather than one of downtown Seoul's hippest bars. Located on the fifth floor of a run-down building in the industrial Euljiro neighborhood, Seendosi can be a bit tough to find, its discreet first-floor sign barely noticeable, the four flights of steps dark. You might not even know there's a bar at the top until you see the neon glow of the entrance. It's no surprise that the bar's owners, photographer Lee Yunho and artist Lee Byoungjae, run a surreally appointed establishment with eccentric 1980s furniture, vintage trinkets, "found" items

and plenty of neon. On a weeknight, the crowd is a mix of local artists, musicians and writers but on the weekend, you'll find people of all sorts. Seendosi often hosts indie music performances, too.

During the summer, you can sit on the roof, where there's an electronic waterfall and views of the surrounding cityscape. You'll find cocktails, beers and wine on the menu, but this bar's more about the atmosphere.

📍 31, Eulji-ro 11-gil, Jung-gu
📞 070-8631-4557
🌐 seendosi.com
💲

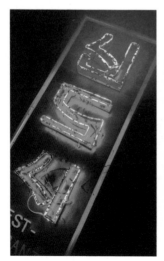

Jean Frigo

An Instagram favorite, Jean Frigo looks like a fruit store at first glance. It's not. Taking its name from owner Jang Ji-ho's name and the French word for refrigerator, this bar in the gritty Dongdaemun district does, in fact, have plenty of fruit and what would seem to be walk-in refrigerator doors on the first floor. Don't be fooled, though—the doors are the entrance to the second-floor speakeasy. The fun doesn't stop there. You use retro phone booths instead of waiters to place orders, and the plush seating faces the walls instead of the center. This could have easily turned gimmicky, but the simple elegance of the exposed concrete interior and the excellence of the fruit cocktails made with traditional Korean alcohol make Jean Frigo anything but.

9-8, Toegye-ro 62-gil, Jung-gu
02-2275-1933
instagram.com/jeanfrigo_official
$$

Mr. Ahn's Craft Makgeolli 안씨막걸리

Hidden in the backstreets of Gyeongnidan, Mr. Ahn's Craft Makgeolli is one of the most talked-about names in the Korean traditional alcohol scene. Former politician Ahn Sang-hyun opened the brewery and gastropub in 2013; he chose the neighborhood because it was the birthplace of Korea's craft beer scene. With a modern design and an extensive menu, the bar offers a wide range of less common *makgeolli*, with everything from Lee Sang-hun Takju from Asan at 19 percent to Song Myung-sub Makgeolli from Taein at 6 percent. A chart helps you choose the right one for you. Unlike most *makgeolli* bars that serve simple dishes, the pub grub here changes seasonally and is more akin to what you'd find in the fine dining scene. The chefs beautifully present their dishes on traditional Korean china, just another reason why Mr. Ahn's is a cut above the rest.

> 📍 61, Hoenamu-ro 13ga-gil, Yongsan-gu
> 📞 010-9965-5112
> 🌐 facebook.com/ahnmakgeolli
> ⓢ ⓢ

Magpie

You can't tell the story of craft beer in Korea without talking about Magpie. Though craft beers are now all the rage, with even convenience stores offering decent selections of craft brews, there was a time—not so long ago, in fact—that local mass-produced beers dominated the market. Magpie was one of a handful of players who helped end that stranglehold. Opened in 2011 by four expats with an interest in homebrewing, Magpie brews American-style craft beers that creatively use local ingredients. Many of their creations pay tribute to the island of Jeju, where the beer is brewed. Magpie also serves some delicious pizza. They aim to "spread good beer and the culture of craft across the country" like the bird that is their namesake.

Magpie operates a tasting room and a basement space in the hip Gyeongnidan district, the birthplace of Korea's craft beer scene. On a warm summer night, you might find it hard to find a seat, but don't worry—you can buy their offerings in cans and bottles, too.

> 📍 244-1, Noksapyeong-daero, Yongsan-gu
> 📞 02-749-2703
> 🌐 www.magpiebrewing.com
> ⑤

Alice

This innovative speakeasy in Cheongdam-dong serves up delicious cocktails against an elegant backdrop. Inspired by Lewis Carroll's famed 1865 novel, Alice makes subtle reference to the children's classic throughout. There's a white rabbit sign that points in the direction of the bar, motifs from the novel embroidered into napkins and cocktails named after characters in the book.

Though drinks are a bit on the expensive side, starting at around KRW 25,000 with a cover charge of KRW 10,000, Alice does more than just ply you with alcohol. It provides an experience with every drink. Order the Alice Boutique, for instance, and have your grapefruit gin and tonic arrive in a cloud of nitrogen. Take a seat at the bar and strike up a conversation with one of Alice's witty bartenders—they're known for their humor as well as their delicious cocktails.

📍 47, Dosan-daero 55-gil, Gangnam-gu
📞 02-511-8420
🌐 facebook.com/alicecheongdam1
$ $ $

Cobbler

A quiet whisky and cocktail bar housed in a *hanok*, Cobbler is a hidden gem in the up-and-coming Naeja-dong neighborhood. Owner and respected bar man Robin Yoo opened the space in 2017 after renovating it himself, traveling to Japan to pick out the bar's antique furniture and silverware. Yoo says he opened the bar out of nostalgia for traditional Korea. The magical ambiance of the bar makes it a popular after-dinner spot for the employees working in nearby embassies.

There is no menu at the bar but the knowledgeable bartenders can recommend a drink for you based on the flavors you enjoy. Every guest is served a small cobbler pie upon entrance. On special occasions, Yoo likes to serve oysters topped with pomegranate seeds, too. Need something strong? Yoo recommends the signature Bread Peat, a peaty whiskey cocktail served with a toast garnish.

- 📍 16, Sajik-ro 12-gil, Jongno-gu
- 📞 02-733-6461
- 🌐 facebook.com/BarCobbler
- ⓢ ⓢ

© Cobbler

© Cobbler

Hopscotch

This gastro pub in a quiet corner of Seochon is the perfect place for a rainy evening. The *hanok* bar blends seamlessly into the neighborhood, an area with many traditional-style homes. Drinks of choice include imported Belgian beers and craft beers from the local brewery Hand and Malt. The exceptional menu sublimates the drinking experience. The duck fat fries are a favorite, while others recommend the Jambalaya Pasta.

The courtyard offers fantastic views of the sky on sunny days, but Hopscotch becomes magical in the rain, when the sound of the raindrops falling on the roof and the intense smell of the wood bring the *hanok* to life.

📍 14-1, Hyoja-ro 7-gil, Jongno-gu
📞 02-722-0145
🌐 facebook.com/Hopscotch.kr
💲💲

Jong3-*pocha* 종3포차

Although commonly portrayed on Korean television and in movies, drinking at a *pojangmacha* or *pocha* —a tent bar—is less prevalent than you might imagine, especially among younger people. The group of *pocha* outside of Jongno 3-ga Station, affectionately called Jong3-*pocha*, is an exception. These drinking establishments remain in vogue, helped along by the gentrification of the nearby Ikseon-dong neighborhood and the area's long history of being LGBT-friendly.

You might need a Korean friend to help you navigate this group of orange and red tents, but here are a few tips: soju is the drink of choice, you must order food if you'd like a seat, and many *pocha* serve an array of seafood the non-initiated may consider "strange." Don't forget to bring some cash with you, too.

> 📍 33, Donhwamun-ro 11-gil, Jongno-gu
> ⓢ

Seoul at Night with
DJ Yuzo and DJ Nunchi

Founded in 2016, Seoul Community Radio (SCR) is an online platform that showcases Korean underground musicians, especially independent DJs and producers. Despite their short history, they've contributed enormously to the local music scene, even collaborating with the likes of Resident Advisor and Boiler Room. DJ Yuzo and DJ Nunchi of SCR's Contents Team break down Seoul's nightlife and its music scene and share what a night out looks like for them.

How would you describe nightlife in Seoul to someone who's never been here?

Yuzo: There's a lot to explore. Artists don't really limit themselves to one kind of music. There's a lot of experimentation—in one night, you can go to three clubs and get completely different genres in each one. I think people are ready to accept that kind of diversity here.

How do you think the nightlife scene here has changed?

Yuzo: I started going clubbing when I was about 21. Back then, I didn't have any taste in music so I just went out to have fun with friends. I went to Cocoon in Hongdae—a beginner club for people who had just become legal adults.

Nunchi: I didn't grow up here so I can only give my first impressions of the present. One of the first things that made me feel welcome was becoming involved with the local queer community. I found out about Shade, which is a regular party that happens at Cakeshop. It's very LGBT-friendly and the DJs are part of that community as well.

When you have friends visit, where do you take them?

Nunchi: Itaewon, because there are a lot of good clubs in one area. I keep getting stuck in this bubble of the same four clubs. Because of the connections I have, it's so easy to go the same places like Cakeshop, Contra, Pistil and Soap.

Yuzo: Seoul is crazy, you know? In one street, you can go to six clubs at least.

Where do you go when you want to get out of that bubble?

Yuzo: In Hongdae and Hapjeong, there are Henz, MODECi and Dip. The last one is a small, cozy warehouse kind of club.

Nunchi: Oh, if we're talking experimental music, there's Constant Value.

Yuzo: If we're going for experimental techno, really deep, dark stuff, then you should go to Constant Value.

Are there DJs that you follow?

Nunchi: I really like C'est Qui. They're a duo made up of DJs Naone and Closet Yi. They played when Boiler Room was here. I look up to them. They play quality music. They're also the only female DJs that I really see play regularly at the places I go. Before their set, they have so much fun and dance, but once it's their time to play, they're totally focused.

Yuzo: I would say DJ Sin. She's also a female DJ and she's been DJing forever. She plays techno and tech-house stuff.

Korean women are expected to retire from certain things at a certain age. Do you worry about that at all? Do you think you could work in underground music when you're in your forties, for instance?

Yuzo: Actually, my sister asks me about this. The reality is we cannot be simply DJs. It would be very hard to be successful. No one ever says, "Oh, you're girls, so you can't play," but I don't know how to fit in and they don't know how to get me involved. I think the music scene in Korea is pretty male-dominated.

Nunchi: I think this is true not just in Korea, though. Of course it happens here, but anywhere you go, people are surprised when there are famous female DJs.

Do you guys also like to drink?

Yuzo: Oh my god, yes. We're crazy. We just do shots and go to the club, that's it. We're not really the barhopping type.

Nunchi: Yeah, we just drink at convenience stores. Convenience store soju—just put a straw in it, sip it really quickly and go. That's our routine.

Written by **Hahna Yoon**

Nature

Wherever you are in Seoul, you never have to travel far to get to the great outdoors. Few metropolises integrate their surroundings as fully as the Korean capital. You can find plenty of hiking opportunities even in the heart of the city itself.

Following the principles of feng shui, Seoul's founders placed the city in a basin with mountains to the north and a river to the south. Though the city has transformed and grown in the ensuing six centuries, its topography has changed very little. The forested mountains that ring Seoul's old downtown and provide landmarks serve as the city's lungs and offer refuge to the worn and weary. More intense hikes await in the rugged granite peaks of Bukhansan National Park, a mere subway's ride from downtown. The Hangang River, meanwhile, continues to carry life into the capital, just as it has done for centuries.

Seoulites have been busy creating their own outdoors, too. The city's beautiful parks not only give residents a place to rest and play, but also embrace local history and culture, sometimes in inspiring ways. But don't take our word for it—get out there and explore.

Namsan Mountain 남산

In the days of Joseon, Namsan Mountain marked the southern limit of Seoul. Now, the peak sits in the heart of the city. Topped by the iconic N Seoul Tower, the mountain may even be the capital's most recognized landmark.

Topping out at just 262 meters above sea level and crisscrossed by walking trails, Namsan Mountain makes for an easy, leisurely walk. You have plenty of options, too—you can hike through forests of gnarled red pines, stroll along Seoul's historical city wall, take in the views from N Seoul Tower or shoot photos of the cityscape from observation decks built on scenic spots along the paths. Not in the mood to walk? No worries—there are buses and even a cable car that will take you to the top, too.

To get the most out of the mountain, try the Namsan Mountain Circuit Trail, or Namsan Sunhwan Sanchaek-gil. Taking about three hours to complete, the 9.8 km network of trails connects many of the mountain's leading attractions, including N Seoul Tower, the old city walls and Baekbeom Plaza.

📍 105, Namsangongwon-gil, Yongsan-gu (N Seoul Tower)

📞 02-3455-9277, 9288

🌐 www.seoultower.co.kr

Bugaksan Mountain 북악산

Bugaksan Mountain played a critical role in determining the royal capital's development. Joseon's first palace, Gyeongbokgung, was built directly in front of the peak. It was the starting point for the city's wall, too. The office of the Korean president sits at its foot today.

Following a failed attempt in 1968 by North Korean commandos to assassinate the South Korean president, the government declared the mountain off limits to the public for security reasons. Though it reopened the mountain in 2006, hikers must present identification, photos are restricted to designated areas, and you must stick to the trail. Protected from human activity, the mountain's forests have flourished. Hikers can enjoy the best-preserved sections of Seoul's old city walls here, too.

The most popular trail begins at Malbawi Information Center near Waryong Park in the east and ends at Changuimun Gate in the west. Taking two hours to complete, the trail follows the old city wall, passing along the way Sukjeongmun Gate. A bit more wild is the so-called Kim Sinjo Route, a trail that follows the tracks of the 1968 North Korean commando team as it attempted to escape through the mountain.

Bugaksan Mountain is also home to one of Seoul's best kept secrets, the Baeksasil Valley, where salamanders, Dybowski's frogs, Oriental fire-bellied toads and even the odd wild boar thrive in cool mountain streams sheltered by a thick forest canopy.

> ⚲ 192, Waryonggongwon-gil, Jongno-gu (Waryong Park)

Inwangsan Mountain 인왕산

Shamanists consider Inwangsan Mountain to be one of the country's most sacred spots. Indeed, the mountain's temples, shrines and altars and fantastic formations of rock, combined with the chanting, candle-lighting, incense-burning and bell-ringing, generate an otherworldly vibe that blankets the entire peak.

Joseon-era landscape painters loved the mountain, too. The 18th century artist Jeong Seon famously captured the peak after the rain, clouds and mist shrouding its granite cliffs.

The most popular trail begins at Sajik Tunnel and follows the old city wall to the peak, which tops out at 339 meters. From the peak, you can follow the wall down to Changuimun Gate in Buam-dong. The trail affords stunning views of downtown Seoul, especially at night.

Inwangsan Mountain's most important shamanist shrine is Guksadang, a simple wooden hall on the southern slope where shamanist rites, or *gut*, are regularly held. Just above Guksadang is Seonbawi, a surreally anthropomorphic outcrop of granite in front of which supplicants offer prayers. On the lower slope of the western side of the mountain is the recently restored Suseongdong Valley, a popular scenic spot since Joseon times.

> 29, Inwangsan-ro 1-gil, Jongno-gu
> (start of the trail)

Hangang Park 한강공원

The Hangang River cuts a 497.5-kilometer-long, 1-kilometer-wide swath through the heart of Seoul, bisecting the city along an east-west axis into the older, grittier north and the newer, posher south. Aside from being an important social dividing line, the river also provides world-weary Seoulites space to relax and rejuvenate. Grass fields, bike paths, walking trails, sporting grounds and other leisure facilities line the river for its entire length. From windsurfing and yachting to enjoying instant noodles at the convenience store, Hangang River Park has something for everyone.

Hangang Park is divided into 11 districts. Popular districts include the centrally located Ichon district, which boasts fields of reeds, rapeseed, cosmos flowers and even barley; the Mangwon district, which is close to the popular Hongdae entertainment district; and the Yeouido district, located in the important financial and media center of Yeouido. The Yeouido park not only draws picnickers with its wide grass fields, but also boasts extensive wetlands. Ferries that depart from the Yeouido, Ttukseom and Jamsil districts offer cruises on the river. The cruises are an excellent way to soak in the beauty of the river, especially at night, when the city lights shine bright in the water.

> ⦿ 330, Yeouidong-ro, Yeongdeungpo-gu, (Yeouido district)
>
> ⊕ hangang.seoul.go.kr

Seonyudo Park 선유도공원

From 1978 to 2000, the Hangang River island of Seonyudo was home to one of Seoul's largest water purification plants. When the plant closed in 2000, however, the city began work on transforming the island into a botanical garden that also honored the site's industrial heritage. The resulting Seonyudo Park, completed in 2002, is one of Seoul's finest examples of adaptive reuse, where lily ponds and tree groves freely mingle with concrete pillars covered in ivy and tastefully rusted machinery.

The most photogenic section of the park is the Garden of Transition, where the concrete structures of the purification plant's sedimentation tanks now host trees, flowers and vines of all sorts. Also lovely is the Garden of Green Columns, a meditative garden where lush ivy covers the old concrete pillars of what was an underground water tank.

Mixing the natural with the man-made, Seonyudo is a popular backdrop for photographers and filmmakers. You can reach the park by car by the Yanghwa Bridge or on foot by a beautiful arched footbridge. The pedestrian bridge, designed by a French architect, also offers lovely views of the surroundings.

📍 343, Seonyu-ro, Yeongdeungpo-gu
📞 02-2631-9368
🌐 parks.seoul.go.kr/seonyudo

Haneul Park 하늘공원

Between 1978 and 1993, the area that is now the World Cup Park complex was Seoul's largest garbage dump, a mountain of trash rising 90 meters above sea level. In 1997, however, the city began work to transform the landfill into a set of parks. After stabilizing the site and landscaping it, the city opened the new parks to the public in 2002, just ahead of the FIFA World Cup.

The highest of World Cup Park's constituent parks at nearly 100 meters, Haneul Park is a sprawling, elevated pasture covered in wild grass and crisscrossed by walking trails. Though beautiful throughout the year, it really comes into its own in autumn, when its fields of pampas grass transform into a shimmering, undulating sea of silver. In October, the park hosts the Seoul Eulalia Festival, when lights, lasers and other illuminates turn the fields into a riot of color.

To reach the park, climb the 291-step staircase or take one of the park's electric trams. Thanks to its elevation, the field offers fine views of the Hangang River, Namsan Mountain and even the peaks of Bukhansan National Park.

📍 95, Haneulgongwon-ro, Mapo-gu
📞 02-300-5510

Seoul Forest 서울숲

A low-lying finger of land at the confluence of the Jungnangcheon Stream and Hangang River, Ttukseom has hosted over the centuries a royal hunting ground, a waterworks, a leisure resort, a horse racing track and an athletics park. In 2003, however, city authorities decided to transform the space into an urban forest to rival New York's Central Park or London's Hyde Park. And so Seoul Forest was born, opening its gates in 2005.

The park boasts over 430,000 square meters of forests, wetlands, gardens and grass fields, linked together by a network of walking trails, bike paths and bridges. Though beautiful all year round, the space really shines in spring and autumn, when it becomes a riot of color. In summer, its grassy lawns and shady forests attract crowds of picnicking families. The park is also home to a population of spotted deer, which visitors can feed.

History buffs should check out the Waterworks Museum, formerly Korean Water Works Company, Korea's first waterworks, opened in 1908. Of much more recent vintage is Understand Avenue (p. 38), a collection of shops and restaurants made of recycled containers in front of the forest's entrance.

📍 273, Ttukseom-ro, Seongdong-gu
📞 02-460-2905
🌐 seoulforest.or.kr

Olympic Park 올림픽공원

A giant oasis of green in southwestern Seoul's sprawl of apartments and skyscrapers, Olympic Park is equal parts nature reserve, historic site, sports and leisure facility and cultural space. Built as part of Seoul's preparations to host the 1988 Summer Olympic Games, the park is so large that it even has its own mini-train to help visitors get around. Rugged wilderness it is not, but it's still a great place to get away from it all, especially for people living or visiting the southern half of the city.

Circumnavigating the park on foot takes about three hours. One of the more pleasant trails is a 2.3 kilometer path along Mongchontoseong Fortress, a circuit of defensive earthworks erected by the ancient Baekje Kingdom in the first century BCE. Inside the fortress you'll find the so-called Lonely Tree, a popular subject of photographers, a solitary evergreen standing on an empty grassy field. The park is also home to two excellent museums: the Seoul Baekje Museum, dedicated to the history of the ancient Baekje Kingdom, and the Soma Museum of Art.

Olympic Park's grassy fields and outdoor stadiums often host concerts and music festivals, too.

- 📍 424, Olympic-ro, Songpa-gu
- 📞 02-410-1114
- 🌐 olympicpark.kspo.or.kr

Bukhansan National Park 북한산 국립공원

You might not expect a national park within the city limits. Bukhansan National Park, however, offers nearly 80 square kilometers of mountain majesty, all of it in Seoul and the northern suburb of Uijeongbu. Granite peaks, deep gorges, thick forests, 1,300 species of flora and fauna, over 100 Buddhist temples and hermitages and a Joseon fortress . . . all just a subway's ride away.

The Uiryeong Pass divides the park into two sections—Samgaksan (another name for Bukhansan) Mountain in the south and Dobongsan Mountain in the north. Both halves boast plenty of rugged granite peaks, including Samgaksan Mountain's Baegundae

Peak, the park's highest point at 836 meters above sea level. One granite dome, Insubong Peak, is a popular rock climbing destination. Many of the park's hikes are difficult, and some are even dangerous. Plan ahead.

If challenging cliff faces isn't your thing, try the Bukhansan Dulle-gil, a 71.8-kilometer network of mostly gentle walking trails that skirt the lower slopes of the park. These trails allow everyone to enjoy the splendor of the park, regardless of hiking ability.

⊕ english.knps.or.kr

Shopping

Seoul is a paradise for any avid shopper. Countless blogs and travel guides tout the city's incredible selection of malls and stores saturating neighborhoods like Myeong-dong, Dongdaemun and Hongdae. It is no secret that inbound tourism relies largely on the popularity of Korean shopping exports, with many overseas visitors coming to Korea primarily to browse and buy. You're unlikely to bump into many local residents on a given Saturday in Myeong-dong; the vast majority of shoppers are international, with the area's hundreds of cosmetics stores even employing native foreign-language speakers to assist with the crowds.

Aside from the super-size department stores, sprawling malls and designated shopping districts, however, there are also a wealth of independent stores and markets to suit every taste and budget. Whether you're wanting to find wares by local designers or discover vintage hand-me-downs, you're guaranteed to find it here. Bring an empty suitcase with you—you're going to need it.

Inohjudan

In Oh, founder of the Korean traditional clothing brand Inohjudan, moved her workshop from the vibrant but hectic Hongdae area to Bukchon Hanok Village's Wonseo-dong neighborhood in 2014. Her designs, while strongly rooted in 17th- to 19th-century traditional dress, incorporate many non-traditional materials and motifs, including prints of the beloved American cartoon character SpongeBob SquarePants. Don't expect to buy anything off the rack, though. Oh's designs are bespoke, each one based on a requisite conversation with the customer. The design process takes about two and a half months, and the work isn't cheap, but the results are wearable works of arts.

📍 78, Changdeokgung-gil, Jongno-gu
📞 02-322-7336
🌐 inohjudan.us
$$$

Beaker

"Multi-shops"—stores selling multiple brands spanning clothing to homeware—have exploded in popularity in Seoul. While multi-shops have appeared (and disappeared) in significant numbers over the past few years, Beaker has made a steady name for itself as one of the best.

Beaker offers over 200 local and international contemporary brands like Carhartt, Nohant and Rag & Bone, as well as in-house collections, ranging in price from affordable to very high-end. Collaborations with local designers produce pieces not available anywhere else in Seoul, and seasonal sales see many items offered at more reasonable prices.

While Beaker has branches at department stores across the city, the two independent flagship stores are attractions in their own right, with sleek wood floors and stairs constructed from recycled furniture. The Cheongdam flagship store also boasts its own chic café, offering shoppers a moment's post-spree respite.

Hannam	Cheongdam
♀ 241, Itaewon-ro, Yongsan-gu	♀ 408, Apgujeong-ro, Gangnam-gu
☏ 070-4118-5216	☏ 02-543-1270
⊕ en.beakerstore.com	
⑤~⑤⑤⑤	

Åland

There is likely not a fashion follower's wardrobe in Korea that does not contain at least one piece from Åland. Opened in 2006, Åland is the embodiment of youthful Korean street fashion, offering garments typical of trendy youngsters seen at Seoul Fashion Week and on the streets of Hongdae.

Although varying according to designer, prices are usually reasonable. The stores are home to a wealth of independent Korean brands, as well as famous international names like Cheap Monday and Toms. The larger stores in Sinsa-dong and Hongdae also sell homewares, skincare and makeup. The Hongdae flagship store is an impressive architectural construction split across two buildings, boasting an exhibition space and garden on its fifth floor.

Hongdae

📍 29, Yanghwa-ro 16-gil, Mapo-gu

📞 02-3210-5882

🌐 a-land.co.kr

ⓢ~ⓢⓢ

© Åland

Gentle Monster

Eyewear brand Gentle Monster is well known for its experimental—and often pretty weird—approach to store design. Walking into one of the three Gentle Monster flagship spaces in Seoul, shoppers would be forgiven for mistaking it for a contemporary art museum.

Located in Hongdae, Sinsa-dong and Bukchon Hanok Village, each store runs along its own unique theme, boasting multiple floors of moving geometrical installations, mirrored rooms and abstract sculptures. Gentle Monster's glasses frames and sunglasses can be spotted dotted along inconspicuous shelves.

A pair of Gentle Monster sunglasses will set you back anywhere between $200 and $350 and range in design from interesting to eccentric. The brand also has flagship stores in Shanghai, Beijing, Hong Kong, London, the United States and elsewhere.
(Photos taken at Bukchon store)

Bukchon	Sinsa	Hongdae
📍 92, Gyedong-gil, Jongno-gu	📍 23, Apgujeong-ro 10-gil, Gangnam-gu	📍 54, Dongmak-ro 7-gil, Mapo-gu
📞 070-4895-1287	📞 070-5080-0196	📞 02-3144-0864
🌐 www.gentlemonster.com		

Style Nanda Pink Hotel

This striking pink building in the middle of Myeong-dong is not actually a hotel, but rather a Wes-Anderson-meets-contemporary-retro-chic-inspired store by local fashion brand Style Nanda. The towering structure boasts six launderette-, spa- and hotel lobby-themed floors of makeup, clothes, shoes and accessories, as well as a café and outdoor rooftop terrace.

Founded in 2004, Style Nanda is one of Korea's leading names in young, high-street fashion, and stores across the country offer a selection of Style Nanda-made and branded fashion at the height of youthful trends. Offering a unique shopping experience and plenty of photo opportunities, the Style Nanda Pink Hotel concept proved so popular upon its opening in 2016 that a second branch opened in Bangkok the following year.

Style Nanda also has its own extensive line of cosmetics, 3 Concept Eyes, now one of the most popular Korean make-up brands overseas, and newer sub-brand of clothing, KKXX, all available in-store.

📍 37-8, Myeongdong 8-gil, Jung-gu
📞 02-752-4546
🌐 stylenanda.com
⑤~⑤⑤

216

Havebeenseoul

Havebeenseoul introduces a curated selection of uniquely Korean artworks, crafts and lifestyle products. The art shop offers Korean traditional items such as straw handicraft cases, combs, tableware and lacquerware given a contemporary makeover and contemporary lifestyle items reinterpreted in a traditionally Korean way. You'll find beautiful traditional lacquered boxes with checkered patterns, eco bags designed to look like traditional "lucky pouches," sophisticated reinterpretations of traditional board games, wine goblets made from traditional brassware, steel frame renditions of traditional Korean furniture, ceramic paperknives and fountain pens, mother of pearl defusers, unbreakable silicone lamps shaped like Joseon Dynasty porcelain jars and even gorgeously painted *hwatu* playing cards. The wares aren't cheap, but you'll be getting what you paid for.

The showroom, a renovated home tucked away in a residential corner of the tony Cheongdam-dong district, compliments the collection with its chic minimalism.

> 📍 1F, 17, Bongeunsa-ro 18-gil, Gangnam-gu
> 📞 02-3422-1777
> 🌐 www.havebeenseoul.com
> ⓦ ~ ⓦⓦⓦ

Object

Concept store Object offers a wide range of pottery, stationary, posters, objets d'art, home interior products, clothing, independent publications and other lifestyle goods produced by local independent artists and artisans. It also commissions works for sale under its own brand, which emphasizes responsible consumerism and product longevity. Object notepads and canvas bags, for instance, are built to last, boasting sturdy construction and thoughtful design. The new flagship store in Hongdae, located not far from Hongik University Station, hosts exhibits by local artists and creatives, too.

📍 13, Wausan-ro 35-gil, Mapo-gu
📞 02-3144-7738
🌐 objectlifelab.com
$

Kakao Friends

While not necessarily the place to head for some serious style-hunting, for a cute and kitsch souvenir not available anywhere else, there's arguably nowhere better than the Kakao Friends flagship store in Gangnam and Hongdae.

Kakao Friends is the name given to the official emojis of Kakao Talk, Korea's answer to WhatsApp, and the tiny animations have developed somewhat of a cult following in Korea over the past few years. The Kakao Friends stores offer more than 1,500 items themed along the eight characters, which include a dog, a tiny crocodile, and a suspect-looking peach.

Merchandise at the stores ranges from cushions and pajamas to phone cases, notebooks, mugs and passport holders. While lines at the door were hours long when the shops first opened, most stores are now easily accessible on weekdays. Head to the top floor of the Gangnam Kakao Friends flagship for emoji-themed cakes and coffees.

📍 429, Gangnam-daero, Seocho-gu
📞 02-6494-110
🌐 kakaofriends.com
💲

© Haut Collection

Ssamzigil

The sheer number of trinkets for sale in Seoul can seem overwhelming at times, and it's often hard to distinguish the better options from the potential knockoffs. The Ssamzigil permanent market offers a fantastic selection of products from good-quality Korean brands and designers.

The market is spread across four open-air floors encircling a small outdoor plaza, and its winding passageways are lined with independent stores selling everything from hats and watches to scented candles, contemporary *hanbok* and leather goods. Prices are fixed, but generally reasonable, and you can purchase with the knowledge that you are investing in something locally made.

Ssamzigil lies just off of Insa-dong Art Street, famous in Seoul for its souvenir and *hanbok* shops and collection of traditional *hansik* restaurants. Enjoy a wander around Insa-dong after your Ssamzigil shopping spree.

📍 44, Insadong-gil, Jongno-gu
📞 02-736-0088
🌐 ssamzigil.co.kr

Gwangjang Vintage Clothing Market

Gwangjang Market is one of the best-known traditional markets in the city. Its ground floor offers hundreds of stalls selling Korean fabrics and affordable wares, and its alleys are lined with rows of street food vendors cooking up typical Korean drinks and snacks.

It's on the second floor, however, where things get interesting for fashion enthusiasts. Dozens of tightly-packed vintage clothing booths—each operated by an independent seller—are lined wall-to-wall with worn but mostly branded jackets, jeans, jumpers, shoes and handbags. While not as cheap as a typical second-hand shop, those looking for a vintage staple piece or rare fashion find will enjoy rummaging through the items here. Bring cash, as merchants rarely accept credit cards, and be prepared to haggle.

📍 88, Changgyeonggung-ro, Jongno-gu
📞 02-2267-0291
🌐 www.kwangjangmarket.co.kr

Bamdokkaebi Night Market

Sponsored by the Seoul Metropolitan Government, the Bamdokkaebi Night Market brings together local designers and sellers for a shopping-entertainment fest during the warmer months of each year. Open every Friday and Saturday evening from March to October at locations across Seoul, these night markets offer everything from affordable, handmade jewelry and accessories to food trucks and live music performances. Those looking for a small, locally made souvenir from their time in Seoul will likely find it here.

Head to the Bamdokkaebi Market right next to Banpo Bridge to also enjoy the Banpo rainbow musical fountain, which operates sporadically throughout the evening in the spring and summer. We recommend arriving early; the markets tend to get crowded around 8 p.m.

> Banpo Hangang Park, Dongdaemun Design Plaza, Oil Tank Culture Park, Cheonggye Plaza, Yeouido Hangang Park
>
> ⊕ bamdokkaebi.org

Experiences

"When in Rome, do as the Romans do." In Seoul, this means you'll be in for a world of new experiences. Though some may seem exotic, at least at first, you may find they stem from a familiar place. Some experiences can be opportunities to learn. Take a *makgeolli* brewing class and you'll soon realize the depth of the drink's ties to Korean history. Bathing at a *jjimjilbang* can teach you more about Korean culture than any museum. Just do as the Seoulites do to enrich your time in the city.

Cooking & Other One-Day Classes

With Korean cuisine receiving greater attention overseas, more visitors are taking Korean cooking classes than ever before. If you'd like to learn how to make kimchi, the **Seoul Kimchi Academy** in Myeong-dong is a well-established name. If you'd like to learn a wider selection of Korean dishes, though, contact **O'ngo Food Communications**. With high reviews across the board, the company offers intimate, locally led group tours as well as classes for students of every level. It even has options for those keeping halal. As classes and tours fill up quickly, make sure to reserve in advance. Vegetarians and those interested in Buddhist dishes can check out the **Korean Temple Food Center** near Insa-dong. Though most classes are held in Korean on a monthly basis, there are classes in English on Saturdays.

If you enjoy hands-on experiences, you'll be glad to know there are many DIY courses and one-day classes in Seoul. Programs include making couple rings, painting ceramics and designing your own scent. Check out One More Trip (www.onemoretrip.net), Seoul's official guide for local tours and experiences.

Makgeolli & Soju Making

To truly understand traditional Korean alcohol, you have to understand its history and how it's made. **The Sool Gallery**, located in Gangnam, is a great place to start. Expert guides walk you through different types of traditional Korean alcohol, offering you a dozen or so samples along the way. If you're looking for a more hands-on approach, expat-operated **The Sool Company** runs a variety of programs on everything from brewing *makgeolli* to tasting tours and day trips that examine traditional Korean alcohol in rural Korea. The company's classes and its website are friendly, informative

and accessible. Another good option, albeit one less accessible to non-Korean speakers, is **Samhae Soju**, located in Samcheong-dong. Run by brew master Kim Taek-sang, this brewery not only produces Samhae Soju, a high-end artisanal spirit, the brewing of which has been designated by the government as an intangible cultural property, but offers classes on brewing, too. Though Kim speaks little English, he is one of the city's top authorities on traditional alcohol. As long as you bring an interpreter with you, you'll learn a lot from him.

Festivals & Fairs

From performance art to crafts and instant noodles, there's a festival for every topic under the rainbow. Festival season in Seoul kicks off in spring with floral festivals such as the **Yeongdeungpo Yeouido Spring Flower Festival**, but goes into full drive in May and June with major music festivals such as **Seoul Jazz, Greenplugged Seoul** and **Ultra Music Festival**. Although Buddha's Birthday is celebrated according to the lunar calendar, the **Lotus Lantern Festival** held in its honor usually falls in May and features a parade down Jongno and thousands upon thousands of paper lanterns. Another festival of lights, the **Seoul Lantern Festival,** is held on the Cheonggyecheon in autumn.

In October, the city hosts its signature **Seoul Street Arts Festival,** formerly the Hi Seoul Festival. The festival transforms downtown Seoul into a huge stage with sometimes spectacular and often quirky performances by street theater troupes from around the world. Another autumn highlight is the **Grand Mint Festival,** a music festival bringing together plenty of Korean indie pop bands.

Other fun festivals include the **Seoul Kimchi Festival, Seoul Design Festival,** the **Craft Trend Fair** and the **Seoul Performing Arts Festival.** For quirky, off-the-beaten-track festivals, try the **"Do Nothing" Competition, Korea International Ramen Fair** or **Water Gun Festa.** Seoul's LGBTQ community's biggest event, the **Seoul Queer Culture Festival,** is held in July.

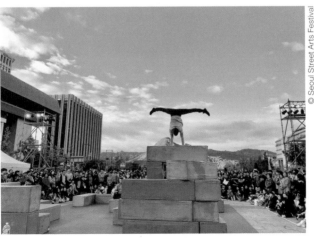

© Seoul Street Arts Festival

Templestay

Operated by the Jogye Order of Korean Buddhism, Korea's largest Buddhist denomination, the Templestay describes itself as "a joyful journey to find the true happiness within yourself." The program allows you to experience life at one of the order's many Buddhist temples throughout the country, including several in Seoul.

For a short glimpse of the monastic experience, look into a one-day program, which can mean anything from lessons on Buddhist crafts to temple tours. In Seoul, **Gilsangsa** in Seongbuk-dong and **Bongeunsa** in Gangnam are known for their wealth of one-day activities in English.

For a more in-depth experience, try the overnight programs and venture outside the city. Though many of the programs follow a similar routine—you wake up early, meditate, have tea with the monks and eat temple food—the program's focus may vary from temple to temple. If you're into martial arts, for instance, try the Templestay program at Gyeongju's **Golgulsa**, where the monks practice *sunmudo*, a meditative martial art.

See the Templestay website for a list of host temples and reservation information.

🌐 www.templestay.com

Jjimjilbang 찜질방

Made popular in the United States by late-night TV host Conan O'Brien, going to a *jjimjilbang* is a favorite local activity. A *jjimjilbang* is a gender-segregated bathhouse where visitors can shower, bathe, sweat and get exfoliated—normally in that order. Locals swear that alternating between baths of different temperatures not only relaxes, but also helps to improve circulation. Most *jjimjilbang* have additional facilities such as restaurants, massage chairs, nail and beauty parlors, co-ed rooms for watching television and sleeping quarters. One such *jjimjilbang* is Yongsan's **Dragon Hill Spa & Resort,** popular with international visitors. Guests praise **Siloam Sauna,** near Seoul Station, for its central location and cleanliness.

Many women say females-only *jjimjilbang* are often much cleaner than mixed-gender facilities. **Spa Lei** in Apgujeong-dong is a top pick.

If you'd like to get exfoliated as part of your experience but would prefer a gentler scrub-down, make sure to tell your exfoliator *"sal-sal hae-ju-se-yo"* (go easy on me).

© Su Noraebang

Noraebang 노래방

When done right, going to a *noraebang* can be one of the funniest things you can do in Korea. A *noraebang*—literally, a "singing room"— is a private karaoke room visitors can rent out by the hour. Popular hours are from 11 p.m. to 4 a.m., when drunken revelers come to finish out their night. The song lists include all your favorite Korean and English standards; nowadays, hits in Chinese, Tagalog and other languages are commonplace, too. Although drinks and snacks are often available, many partiers sneak in drinks discreetly.

For a premium experience, be on the lookout for a luxury *noraebang*. These places have much cleaner facilities, a wider selection of songs and are often kid-friendly. One of the best known is **Su Noraebang** in Hongdae, easily recognized by its tall glass windows that face the public.

Solo singers can also find coin-*noraebangs* in arcades that'll charge you by the song in a small booth.

Baseball Games

"America's pastime" is popular throughout East Asia, too, including Korea. The passion shown by Korean fans for their team often impresses non-Korean observers. The energy is powered in part by the plethora of food and drinks available at the stadiums before and during the games. Fried chicken—washed down by beer—is the Korean baseball fan's fuel of choice. Food and drink prices are blissfully reasonable—unlike in the United States, concession stands don't price gouge fans. Regular season games rarely sell out. Just show up an hour before the game and buy your ticket at the gate.

Seoul's two main stadiums are at opposite ends of the city: Guro-gu and Jamsil. **Gocheok Sky Dome,** home of the Nexen Heroes, is nice on rainy days because of its dome, but **Jamsil Baseball Stadium,** home of the Doosan Bears and LG Twins, has larger crowds and more of a party vibe. There are cheerleaders, performances and proud fans that know all the lyrics and motions to the cheers, so even if you're completely ignorant of baseball, it's still fun to people-watch.

© CJ E&M

eSports

Though eSports may feel like the future in most countries, it's today in Seoul. Fiercely competitive video game matches draw crowds of thousands and generate millions of dollars in corporate sponsorships. You can take in the spectacle in several ways. The most exciting is to plan your trip to coincide with a large eSports event. The 2014 League of Legends Championship drew 40,000 people to the World Cup Stadium. **Seoul OGN e-Stadium** in Sangam-dong and **Nexon Arena** in Gangnam compete for the title as the city's best eSports stadium. Hosting a game every Wednesday, Thursday and Saturday, the OGN e-Stadium's facilities can hold up to 1,000 guests. It feels a bit more modern, too. On the other hand, Nexon Arena, designed by game developers themselves, is a more intimate venue of 400 seats. Tickets usually range from free to KRW 5,000. The bigger matches are called in English as well as Korean.

Small House Big Door

Accommodations

Seoul's accommodation scene used to be a tad limited, presenting a stark choice between major international luxury chains and cheap local inns, with a few mid-priced hotels in popular tourist area.

Such is the case no longer. Sure, the luxury hotels and cheap inns are still there, but joining them are a generation of boutique hotels that mix comfort and creativity. Designers are turning the city's history—disused commercial properties, colonial era homes and even older motels—into spaces that are travel destinations in their own right. Often located in some of Seoul's hottest neighborhoods, this new batch of hotels also make great base camps to explore the city.

In addition to the new, Seoul's accommodation scene also boasts the very old. In historical neighborhoods such as Bukchon, a few old tile-roofed homes, or *hanok*, have been repurposed as boutique hotels and guest houses. These offer guests a more intimate stay and an unmatched opportunity to experience the elegance of traditional Korean culture.

Hotel Cappuccino 호텔 카푸치노

Located in the heart of Gangnam, the glitzy, brash face of the new Seoul, Hotel Cappuccino bills itself as an "urban lifestyle destination," a "place for beautiful people who believe in value-based travel." Guests are invited to take part the hotel's "Shared Values" projects, fun programs that aim to save water and reduce waste through recycling and reducing water usage. The rooms are hip, minimalist and monochromatic—it's like sleeping in a monochrome painting. Got a dog? Try the Bark Room, with custom pet beds, a pet bath, pet toys, poo bags and more. The hotel restaurant offers your favorite Vietnamese, Japanese and Thai comfort foods as well as Korean dishes; the café serves coffee from renowned Seoul coffeehouse Anthracite; and the rooftop bar—Seoul's first gintoneria, for those keeping score at home—not only serves a healthy selection of classic and premium gins, but also offers some of the best views in the city.

- 155, Bongeunsa-ro, Gangnam-gu
- 02-2038-9500
- Twin room from KRW 130,000
- hotelcappuccino.co.kr

Small House Big Door 스몰 하우스 빅 도어

Hidden in a relatively quiet corner of the bustling Myeong-dong commercial district, Small House Big Door is more than just a boutique hotel. It's a cultural space, with a gallery on the first floor where you'll find regular exhibits by local artists and designers. Design studio Design Methods transformed a 50-year-old office building into a 25-room celebration of minimalism and the color white. The designers used 3D printers to create the furnishings and signage using open source designs, so if you like what you see, just download the schematics and recreate it at home (assuming you have a 3D printer). The first-floor bistro serves good salads, burgers and pasta dishes, and you can enjoy a nightcap in the rooftop lounge.

- 6, Namdaemun-ro 9-gil, Jung-gu
- 02-2038-8191
- Double room from KRW 93,500
- smallhousebigdoor.com

A.MASS Hotel 에이메스 호텔

The A.MASS Hotel is a friendly little place located just across the street from the spectacular Changdeokgung Palace, a UNESCO World Heritage Site. The rooms, though small, feel much bigger than they are thanks to efficient design—from the mini-fridge to the walk-in shower, everything has a purpose. The hotel, a remodeled office building, boasts a minimalist, almost urban decor with plenty of exposed concrete and white walls. Located in the heart of the old city, just a short walk from major tourist destinations such as the royal palaces, Bukchon Hanok Village, Insa-dong and Daehangno, the place also makes a good base camp for urban exploration. As an added bonus, the hotel lends bicycles to guests for free. There's a restaurant on the first floor, but the real gem is the rooftop bar, where you can enjoy a pizza, pasta or salad with a glass of wine and views of Changdeokgung Palace.

📍 11, Yulgok-ro 10-gil, Jongno-gu
📞 02-744-1271
🌐 Double room from KRW 65,000

Nagwonjang Hotel 낙원장

Iksundada, a studio engaged in urban rejuvenation projects in the historical Ikseon-dong district, renovated an old motel built in the 1980s, transforming it into a chic boutique hotel that celebrates youthful creativity as well as the neighborhood's past. Collaborating with local artists and designers, Iksundada has created a space that manages to combine modern sophistication and analog sensibility, from the original tile in the glass-enclosed lobby to the classic LP players in the guest rooms. Rooms have no TV sets, further accentuating the analog vibe. The rooftop lounge bar overlooks Ikseon-dong's many alleys of *hanok* homes—it's like gazing down on a sea of tile roofs. Guests can not only enjoy fine dining in the hotel's dining room or a coffee and scone in the café, but also receive discounts at some of Ikseon-dong's other restaurants, bars and shops.

> 📍 25, Supyo-ro 28-gil, Jongno-gu
> 📞 02-742-1920
> 💲 Double room from KRW 65,000

© Nagwonjang Hotel

Rakkojae 락고재

Though historical Bukchon Hanok Village has several *hanok* accommodations, Rakkojae is in a league of its own. In 2003, master artisan Chung Young-jin restored this 130-year-old home, transforming it into a boutique hotel that is not only a place to stay, but also a space where you can experience the elegance and charm of old Korea. To pass through Rakkojae's front gate is to return to a simpler, slower, more tranquil era. Everything about Rakkojae is an exercise in traditional sophistication, from the pine and bamboo garden in the central courtyard to the natural jade flooring of the most expensive room, the Master Bedroom. While a simple

Korean or continental breakfast is provided complimentary, you'd do well to pay for dinner, too—the three dinner options are as beautiful as they are delicious. Give the natural mud sauna a try, too. Rakkojae also offers several cultural services, including opportunities to try traditional clothing, kimchi-making classes and performances of traditional music. As there are only five rooms, book your stay early.

> 📍 49-23, Gyedong-gil, Jongno-gu
> 📞 02-742-3410
> Ⓦ Master Bedroom KRW 275,000
> 🌐 rkj.co.kr

Creative House 창신기지

Design studio Z_Lab took a dilapidated, 80-year-old *hanok* home in a sketchy alley of the gritty Changsin-dong district and turned it into a cozy rental house that brings together traditional beauty and contemporary style. This hidden hideaway boasts custom-made Scandinavian furniture by Kaare Klint, lighting by lifestyle brand Limas and fabrics by local design house Kitty Bunny Pony. Guests can enjoy a barbecue in the courtyard, which also has an outdoor tub in which you can take a relaxing bath under the open sky. Creative House is a popular option for parties, too. Nearby attractions include the sprawling Dongdaemun Market, the futuristic Dongdaemun Design Plaza and the eastern section of Seoul's old city wall. Creative House has helped rejuvenate the alleyway, too, taking over another nearby *hanok* and a run-down inn and turning them into Craft Base, a gastro pub and exhibition space.

- 31, Jongno 48-gil, Jongno-gu
- 0504-0904-2002
- KRW 250,000
- creativehouse.co.kr

Nook Seoul 눅서울

Located on the southern slope of Namsan Mountain, the Huam-dong neighborhood has many Japanese-style homes from the early 20th century, a legacy of the colonial era, when the area was a residential district for Japanese settlers. Seoul National University architecture professor Kim Seunghoy has transformed one such home, an 80-year-old wooden house, into one of the city's most spectacular accommodations. The carefully coordinated restoration exposed the old house's beautiful wooden frame and original walls and preserved some other tidbits such a cement relief of flowers created by three Japanese brothers who once lived in the house. The historical framework embraces a living environment appointed with work by some of the world's leading furniture makers and lighting designers. There's an island kitchen and dining space on the first floor, while the basement can be used as a space for meditation or yoga. The windows on the third floor offer relaxing views of the surrounding neighborhood. Throughout the house you'll find plenty of vintage items, including the old washing board hanging in the kitchen.

> 📍 6-2, Sowol-ro 2na-gil, Yongsan-gu
> 📞 010-8284-2886
> 💲 KRW 170,000
> 🌐 nookseoul.com

Bidulki House 비둘기하우스

In Malli-dong, a gritty residential district near the overpass-turned-elevated park Seoullo 7017, a woman has turned the cheap inn her grandmother ran into a cozy guesthouse. Bidulki House preserves the structure of the old inn, including its narrow corridors and staircases, but adds tastefully renovated decor and amenities. The rooms are very simple—basically just a wooden door and some simple Korean-style bedding on the floor. But they provide a good night's sleep, and the place just exudes vintage charm. Single and two-person rooms are available. Guests share the shower and bathroom.

The rooftop has views of Seoullo 7017, Seoul Station, Seoul Square and even Namsan Mountain. The café on the first floor is a cozy space in which to enjoy a cup of coffee or tea. Thanks to Seoullo 7017, the surrounding neighborhood is beginning to take off, so you'll find plenty of good cafés and restaurants nearby, too.

📍 9, Mallijae-ro 37-gil, Jung-gu
📞 0507-1458-0125
🅦 Single room KRW 33,000
🌐 bidulkihouse.modoo.at

© Bidulki House

Publisher
Kim Hyunggeun

Writers
Robert Koehler, Hahna Yoon

Contributors
Cynthia Yoo (Dining), Rhiannon Shepherd (Shopping)

Editor
Eugene Kim

Copy editors
Anna Bloom, Lee Kye-hyun

Designer
Cynthia Fernández

All photos by Robert Koehler except:
Robert Michael Evans (p. 172–173, 214–215, 232)
Dylan Goldby (p. 86, 126–127, 170, 183, 185)
John Romain (p. 43 lower right, 96-97, 206–207)
Marco Devon (p. 122–123)
Matthew Parker (p. 227 lower left)
Min Ha (p. 244 upper)
Yonhap News (p. 234)